Title IX

A Brief History
with Documents

Title IX

A Brief History
with Documents

Susan Ware

WAVELAND
PRESS, INC.
Long Grove, Illinois

For information about this book, contact:
Waveland Press, Inc.
4180 IL Route 83, Suite 101
Long Grove, IL 60047-9580
(847) 634-0081
info@waveland.com
www.waveland.com

Cover photo: © John Kropewnicki

10-digit ISBN 1-4786-1881-7
13-digit ISBN 978-1-4786-1881-2

Printed in the United States of America

7   6   5   4   3   2   1

Preface to the 2014 Edition

In June 2012 Title IX turned forty. *Sports Illustrated* put the anniversary on its cover, and major newspapers and media outlets ran features on how the pathbreaking piece of federal legislation had changed the field of athletics. Most of this coverage was justifiably celebratory. After all, since 1972 women's athletic participation at the high school level had risen an astounding 990% and a robust 560% at the collegiate level. The 2012 Summer Olympic games in London, where every delegation but two included a female athlete and women made up 51% of the U.S. team, confirmed the popular image of dedicated and talented female athletes confidently competing alongside men.

For those who dug a little deeper, the picture was not entirely rosy. The most telling statistic was the stubborn persistence of a participation gap between the sexes. Girls made up 49% of high school students, but got only 42% of the participation opportunities. The gap was even wider at the college level, where women made up a substantial majority of students (57%) but were stuck at 43% of the athletic opportunities. Despite fears that women athletes had gained at the expense of men, research from the Women's Sports Foundation showed that men's participation opportunities over the last decade actually increased faster than those for women.

There were many other places where the athletic landscape was far from equal where gender was concerned. Not every outcome was directly linked to Title IX, but all were part of an American sporting culture that still privileged men as participants, administrators and sports industry executives, and fans. Even as women's sporting opportunities expanded at both the amateur and professional level, the number of women coaches plummeted, as men moved into this relatively lucrative new field. Needless to say, the woman who coached a men's team was a rare bird indeed. Women also lagged in the field of sports administration, comprising a tiny minority of athletic directors, sports information officers and conference commissioners. This low representation was matched in the general field of sports media, where the number of women sportswriters and sportscasters hovered around 10%, with the representation of non-white women even lower. Just as discouraging, a survey conducted at the University of Southern California concluded that between 88 and 95% of all sports coverage in the mainstream media was devoted to men.

These competing stances—celebratory or cautionary—on the impact of Title IX and the changes it sparked speak to the perennial question of whether a glass is half full or half empty. In many ways these breakthroughs for women in sport have been truly revolutionary: young women now take sports for granted in a way that would have been impossible just a generation or two ago. At the same time, there is still a long way to go before women and girls reach anything approaching equity in terms of resources, opportunities, and prestige. An especially disturbing trend is the number of schools which are decreasing or dropping physical education classes and interscholastic sports entirely.

Title IX has encouraged a transformational amount of social change and polls show that it enjoys wide popular acceptance. Yet controversy still lurks just below the surface, especially over the question of whether providing more athletic opportunities for girls and women necessarily means taking them away from boys and men. (The short answer: no, it doesn't.) Even though decades have passed since Title IX's passage, it is just as relevant now as it was in 1972. And Title IX will continue to be a necessary legal and educational tool until the playing field is truly level for all participants regardless of sex.

ACKNOWLEDGMENTS

I would like to thank Neil Rowe and all the folks at Waveland Press who believed that this book deserved to continue to reach new generations of students and teachers. It has been a pleasure working with them and I look forward to a long and productive association.

Susan Ware

Preface

The phrase "Title IX" is practically synonymous with women's athletics, but few students understand how recent the revolution in women's sports is or how highly contested the breakthroughs were. This book of documents is the first to address that void for the classroom. Taking as its organizing theme the thirty-seven words of Title IX of the Education Amendments Act of 1972, which outlaws discrimination on the basis of sex in any education program or activity receiving federal funds, it introduces students to a broad range of historical and philosophical questions that stretch far beyond athletics. Since Title IX has touched the lives of practically every elementary, high school, and college student in this country, its story encourages students to think analytically about recent American history through a subject—athletics and gender equity—that is of great personal interest to many of them. Given the controversy about this wide-ranging law, the topic is guaranteed to provoke spirited classroom discussion in courses such as postwar U.S. history, U.S. women's history and women's studies, and the history of sports, as well as the U.S. survey.

Why is the story of Title IX so central to recent U.S. history? The events leading up to Title IX's passage in 1972, and the struggle ever since to figure out how to implement the law fairly, provide both a historical and a timely test case of the interplay between legislative and social change. In addition to its impact on sports, Title IX is very much linked to the fortunes of modern feminism, from its heyday in the 1960s and 1970s to the backlash that followed. At this book's core is the concept of gender equity—what it means when it comes to sports, and by extension, what it means to American society as a whole.

Built on the assumption that students will have only a sketchy idea of what lies behind the phrase "Title IX" but will be primed by their own experiences to learn more, the introduction provides a short history of women's sports before Title IX as well as a concise overview of the early history of the legislation and the struggle for implementation. In addition to describing the benefits and results of the law, the introduction addresses the objections that have been raised, both in the 1970s and more recently, to Title IX's sweeping mandate for change in athletics.

Armed with this background, students can then move forward to key documents from Title IX's history, presented in a generally chronological organization. The documents open with the "back story" before Title IX, then turn to the early years of its implementation. The debate became increasingly polarized in the 1980s and 1990s, with disputes being contested not just within educational institutions but in courts of law. The last part looks more broadly at Title IX and American culture, including issues such as race and homophobia. The documents were carefully chosen to balance the views of policymakers, legislators, and commentators with the voices of individuals whose lives were shaped by the law. To further encourage discussion, the documents present conflicting points of view from every stage of Title IX's history.

The format of the book is designed to facilitate student engagement with Title IX's larger significance. Each document has a short headnote that introduces the topic, identifies the writer or source, and gives enough context so the student will know why the document is important to the larger story. As mentioned, the introduction and the documents are both organized in a generally chronological fashion; a formal chronology at the end of the book lists key dates and developments. The questions for consideration that follow should facilitate lively discussion or class assignments. The literature on sports and Title IX is growing, and the up-to-date selected bibliography offers students a good starting point for further reading.

ACKNOWLEDGMENTS

If students and instructors have as much fun using this book in the classroom as I did putting it together, I will have a bestseller on my hands. I would like to thank Mary Dougherty and Jane Knetzger for making my wish possible. Additional thanks go to associate editor Shannon Hunt and developmental editor Lisa Rothrauff, who were fine sounding boards on matters editorial and procedural. The manuscript was greatly enriched by the comments and expertise of reviewers Susan Hartmann, The Ohio State University; Hayward (Woody) Farrar, Virginia Tech; Mina Carson, Oregon State University; Pamela Grundy, independent scholar; Margaret Caffrey, University of Memphis; Alice Echols, University of Southern California; and Greg Bond, University of Wisconsin. Thank you all, and see you at the gym.

Susan Ware

Contents

PART ONE

Introduction:
Title IX—Thirty-seven
Words That Changed
American Sports

— Women's teams sell candy bars and hold bake sales to pay for travel expenses, while men's teams travel in buses chartered at the school's expense.
— The women's swim team practices after dinner because that is the only time the pool is available.
— When a new gym is built, the old gym is "retired" to the women.
— A woman referee is paid half that of a male referee to officiate in the same game.[1]

Welcome to the pre–Title IX world of women's sports. In 1971, the year before Title IX was passed, fewer than 295,000 girls participated in high school athletics, just 7 percent of the total number of athletes; fewer than 30,000 women competed in intercollegiate athletics, and women's sports received a scant 2 percent of overall athletic budgets. In contrast, by 2001 almost 2.8 million girls participated in high school athletics, representing 41.5 percent of all varsity athletes; more than 150,000 competed at the college level, representing 43 percent of all athletes.[2] While the playing field is still not totally level, women and girls now have far more opportunities to participate in organized athletic activities in their schools and communities than ever before. Athletics, once viewed as a privilege, is now seen as a right.

Over the years, the two words "Title IX" have become practically synonymous with women's athletics. And yet the story is more complicated than just a law and its outcomes. Many of the breakthroughs and successes that the public ascribes to Title IX were as much the product of the broader social changes spurring more equal participation by women and girls in all facets of American life since the 1970s as they were the results of a specific law. It is no coincidence that Title IX was passed in the same year that the Equal Rights Amendment passed Congress, but even if Title IX had not been enacted, there would still have been a dramatic increase in women's participation in sports, precisely because, as sports historian Kathryn Jay noted, "sports had become too important to American society to exclude half the population."[3] Moreover, since athletics has traditionally been segregated by sex, the disparities between men's and women's opportunities were much easier to see once the nation's consciousness was raised by modern feminism. Some discrimination is subtle, almost invisible—not that in athletics.

The events leading up to Title IX's passage in 1972, and the struggle ever since to figure out how to implement the law fairly, demonstrate how athletics became part of the broader political and cultural struggles of the late twentieth century. Title IX also provides a textbook case of the difficulties—and the rewards—of putting abstract principles like equal opportunity and gender equity into concrete, everyday practice.

Even though Title IX is only three decades old, it has a definite history. What Title IX meant in the 1970s is quite different from what it meant in the 1990s or what it means in the twenty-first century, in part because of the incremental changes in the law's implementation, but also because of changes in the broader political climate. By historicizing Title IX's impact and legacy, we are able to trace how the debate over the meaning and implications of the law has changed over time. This debate raises fundamental questions about sports, gender, and modern life. If the playing field is open to women, must women sign on to the prevailing "win at any cost" mentality that structures most sports dominated by men? Is there a contradiction between striving for equality in sports (and society) while also asserting that women are different from men? In times of diminishing resources, how is it possible to promote equity for underrepresented women without taking opportunities away from men? What is the role of the federal government and the courts in fostering social change? On practically every page of this book lurks this question: What is true gender equity when it comes to sports and athletics, and what role has Title IX played in promoting it?

THE PASSAGE AND EARLY YEARS OF TITLE IX

Title IX of the Education Amendments Act of 1972 is only thirty-seven words long and reads in full: "No person in the United States shall, on the basis of sex, be excluded from participation in, be denied the benefits of, or be subjected to discrimination under any education program or activity receiving Federal financial assistance." Supporters of women's educational equity tucked that small provision into an omnibus education law and then deliberately kept a low profile as the entire bill worked its way through Congress. It worked. A Department of Health, Education, and Welfare (HEW) administrator charged with implementing the law observed in 1974, "I suspect that the great majority of men and women who voted for Title IX didn't even know Title IX was in there."[4]

The original impetus behind the legislation was the widespread discrimination that women faced in all aspects of the educational experience, from students to administrators to professors. The law was designed to fill a gap in coverage of the path-breaking Title VII of the Civil Rights Act of 1964, which banned discrimination based on race, sex, national origin, and religion in employment, but did not apply to educational institutions. As Representative Patsy Mink of Hawaii, who was a key supporter of the original legislation, said in 2002, "When it was proposed, we had no idea that its most visible impact would be in athletics. I had been paying attention to the academic issue. I had been excluded from medical school because I was female."[5]

In 1970 and then again in 1971, Representative Edith Green of Oregon, one of the few women in Congress and an education specialist, held extensive hearings that documented the barriers that women faced in higher education, such as state universities requiring a higher grade point average to admit women or arbitrarily capping the percentage of women in certain professional schools. In 1971, Green's draft legislation was one of several bills introduced in the House. Around the same time, Senator Birch Bayh of Indiana, a good friend of the emerging women's movement, drafted similar legislation in the

Senate. In his view, Title IX represented "an important first step in the effort to provide for the women of America something that is rightfully theirs."[6] It took two tries, but after the differing bills were finally reconciled in a Senate-House conference committee, the Education Amendments Act containing Title IX was signed by President Richard Nixon on June 23, 1972.[7]

At the time of the 1971 hearings, Representative Green predicted that the proposed legislation was "probably going to be the most revolutionary thing in higher education in the 1970s."[8] She was right, but not necessarily in the ways that she expected. In the hearings and debate about the law, athletics had been barely mentioned, other than an offhand remark by Senator Bayh that the law would not mean that football teams had to be coeducational. Because athletic programs did not receive federal funding, they did not immediately seem likely targets for enforcement. But as the law was written, it applied to the entirety of an institution receiving federal funds, not just a specific program, which meant that athletics did indeed fall within its purview. And since the disparities in spending on men's and women's athletic programs were so great (for example, in 1973–1974 the University of Washington's men's teams had a budget of $2.5 million, while women's teams received merely $18,000),[9] under the law they had to be addressed.

Implementation of the law got off to a very slow start. Not until 1974 did the Department of Health, Education, and Welfare circulate draft regulations about areas covered by the law, and these were not finalized until 1975. Elementary schools were then given a one-year grace period (high schools, colleges, and universities got three years) to survey their programs and develop strategies to address the problems uncovered.[10] Not until 1979 did HEW promulgate its final guidelines telling schools what standards they would have to meet to show they were in compliance with the law.

As the proposed regulations began to circulate, HEW secretary Caspar Weinberger quipped that he had not realized "that the most important issue in the United States today is intercollegiate athletics."[11] By then, college athletic administrators and some politicians had begun to realize that this new law might have huge implications for athletic business as usual. While feminists and some female physical education leaders welcomed this new governmental activism, male athletic directors forecast gloom and doom for men's sports programs, especially football. Members of Congress attempted to exempt revenue-producing sports from Title IX's coverage in 1974 and 1975, but both these attempts failed, as did all later ones.

In the early days of the law, much discussion centered on whether teams should be coeducational based on skill (the model adopted in elementary and high school physical education classes) and whether women should be eligible to play on men's teams. On the high school and intercollegiate level, a consensus soon emerged that sex-segregated but comparable sports teams were a better model. Did that mean that schools had to spend as much to outfit a female swimmer as they did to equip a male football player? The Javits Amendment in 1974 clarified that question, recognizing that certain sports such as football had higher equipment costs than others and that the resulting disparities were not necessarily the result of discrimination.[12]

From the start, football loomed over all Title IX discussions. Because of its high costs and huge rosters (upward of eighty-five scholarships, plus as many as fifty additional walk-on players), it was usually the biggest item in a school's athletic budget. Football programs enjoyed such a mystique in local communities and on college campuses, to say nothing of in the minds of alums, that they were practically sacrosanct. Football's seeming invincibility was also aided by the myth that football's gate receipts and revenues paid for the rest of a school's athletic program. As Senator Roman Hruska said in congressional hearings in 1975, "Are we going to let Title IX kill the goose that lays the golden eggs in those colleges and universities with a major revenue-producing sport?"[13] This myth was not backed up by facts then, and is not now. For example, analysis of National Collegiate Athletic Association (NCAA) figures from 1977 showed that, of the 475 members with varsity football programs, less than 1 in 5 of these programs achieved revenue at least equal to operating expenses. The remaining 80 percent did not even break even, although this figure was closer to 50 percent in Division I schools (those with the largest athletic budgets, most competitive schedules, and highest attendance at games).[14] "King Football" has continued to cause major challenges for Title IX enforcement ever since.

In many ways, Title IX is a very flexible law. Instead of telling schools what they have to do, it allows them to choose how to accomplish its goals. The law does not mandate equal expenditures for both sexes, nor does it require that equal numbers of men and women participate on teams. Despite claims from conservative opponents, it is not an affirmative action law: It makes no mention of preferences, quotas, or timetables. Like most antidiscrimination laws, it does not offer any funds for implementation of its mandates, and courts have consistently ruled that lack of money is not a sufficient reason for failing to meet the law's goals.[15]

The 1979 regulations (often called the "three-prong test") offered educational institutions three different routes to show that they were in compliance with Title IX. Institutions needed to show only that they were in compliance with one of the three prongs. With small changes and tweaking over the years, these same standards still are the main guiding principles for all Title IX litigation and compliance reviews today.[16]

The first prong requires that participation opportunities for male and female athletes be substantially proportionate to their general enrollment in the educational institution. For example, if male students make up 55 percent of students, then they should receive approximately 55 percent of the athletic opportunities, with the remaining 45 percent allotted to women. This emphasis on proportionality was a compromise. Two other options had been to require that athletic opportunities be split evenly at 50 percent each or that athletic expenditures be equal for the men's and women's programs. At the time, male undergraduates earned significantly more bachelor's degrees than women (56 percent to 44 percent in 1972), so athletic directors probably breathed a sigh of relief when proportionality was chosen, because that goal seemed much easier to reach than 50-50 parity. Ultimately, however, this compromise backfired when women became a majority of college undergraduates by the 1990s.[17]

The two other routes to compliance concern the key issue of "interest" on the part of the underrepresented sex, in this case, women. The second prong requires that a school show that it has a history and a continuing practice of program expansion to meet the interests and needs of women; the third prong requires demonstration that the school's programs "fully and effectively [accommodate]" the interests and abilities of the underrepresented sex.

Why is this issue of interest so critical, and why has it been so contested? Many athletic administrators and even leaders of the NCAA argued that the disparities between men's and women's programs were not necessarily the result of discrimination, but were the result of longstanding societal factors that meant women were less interested in participating in organized sports than men were. Women's sports leaders dismissed this reasoning out of hand in what came to be known as the *Field of Dreams* rationale, following the 1989 movie of that name. As Donna Lopiano of the Women's Sports Foundation said, "I'm asked all the time whether the interests and abilities of women are met. There's never been a question of enough interest. If you build it, they will come."[18]

Over the years the courts have been especially suspicious when schools have tried to blame women's lack of interest for their failure to increase teams and participation rates. As a federal appeals court ruled in *Cohen v. Brown* (1996), "To assert that Title IX permits institutions to provide fewer athletics participation opportunities for women than for men, based on the premise that women are less interested in sports than men, is (among other things) to ignore the fact that Title IX was enacted in order to remedy discrimination that results from stereotyped notions of women's interests and abilities."[19] Vivian Acosta and Linda Jean Carpenter, the leading authorities on the history and implementation of Title IX, pinpointed why the opportunity to participate is so central to the questions of equity and fairness at the heart of the legislation, as well as the underlying issue of resources and money: "If you are not in the game, you don't need a uniform."[20]

As the delay in drafting regulations suggests, for most of the 1970s HEW relied on the goodwill of institutions rather than active government enforcement to move educational institutions toward greater gender equity. Still, amazing progress for women's athletics occurred, with participation rates leaping practically overnight from the oft-cited figure of 1 in 27 to 1 in 9. (See Figures 1 and 2.) As journalist Candace Lyle Hogan observed at the time, "Fueled by an almost chemical interaction of a federal anti–sex discrimination law, the women's liberation movement, and what is called the temper of the times, women's sports took off like a rocket in 1972."[21]

The revival of feminism in the 1960s and 1970s provided a key backdrop for the tremendous energy gravitating toward women's sports. Starting with initiatives like the President's Commission on the Status of Women from 1961 to 1963, the passage of Title VII of the Civil Rights Act of 1964, and the founding of the National Organization for Women in 1966, the movement reached new constituencies when consciousness-raising groups sprang up on campuses and radical feminists staged a protest against the Miss America pageant in 1968. While popular memory credits the decade of the 1960s as an era of social protest and change, the greatest breakthroughs for the women's movement occurred in the 1970s, especially early in the decade. In 1972, after languishing for almost fifty years, the Equal Rights Amendment passed Congress and was sent to the states for

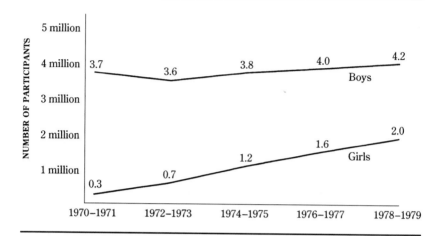

Figure 1. *Number of Boys and Girls Participating in Interscholastic Athletics 1970–1971 to 1978–1979*

Source: National Federation of State High School Associations, *Sports Participation Survey*, 1971, 1973, 1974, 1976, 1978; U.S. Commission on Civil Rights, *More Hurdles to Clear* (Washington, D.C.: U.S. Commission on Civil Rights, 1980), 13.

1972

what looked like quick ratification. That year *Ms.* magazine was launched and Congresswoman Shirley Chisholm ran for president. In 1973, the Supreme Court handed down its landmark decision on abortion in *Roe v. Wade*. Before long, debates over such issues as sex discrimination, pay equity, and equal opportunity were raging not only in the halls of Congress and the chambers of the Supreme Court, but in offices, restaurants, and living rooms across the country. It was not long before many ordinary Americans, not just activists, realized that some of the most glaring examples of gender inequity were found in the field of sports.[22]

WOMEN'S SPORTS IN HISTORICAL PERSPECTIVE

For most of American history, sports have been a male preserve. Competitive athletics were seen as "natural" for men and boys, but somehow "unnatural" or illegitimate for women and girls. As a Connecticut judge said in 1971 when denying girls the right to participate on a boys' high-school cross-country team, "Athletic competition builds character in our boys. We do not need that kind of character in

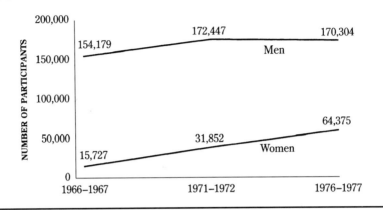

Figure 2. *Number of Men and Women Participating in Intercollegiate Athletics 1966–1967 to 1976–1977*

Source: Comments of the National Collegiate Athletic Association on the Proposed Policy Interpretation of the Department of Health, Education, and Welfare Regarding Application of Its Title IX Regulation to Intercollegiate Athletics, 11; U.S. Commission on Civil Rights, *More Hurdles to Clear* (Washington, D.C.: U.S. Commission on Civil Rights, 1980), 22.

our girls, the women of tomorrow. . . ."[23] Shaped by a popular belief that women's bodies were inherently different from—and weaker than—men's, women's sports developed along a path similar to that of segregated schools in the South before the 1954 *Brown v. Board of Education* Supreme Court decision: separate and definitely unequal.

Just because society discouraged girls and women from being physically active does not mean that they meekly sat on the sidelines in their starched dresses and crinolines. Nineteenth-century author Louisa May Alcott stated forthrightly, "Active exercise was my delight. . . . No boy could be my friend till I had beaten him in a race, and no girl if she refused to climb a tree, leap fences, and be a tomboy." In the 1890s, temperance leader Frances Willard learned to ride a bicycle and then wrote a book about the experience. In the 1930s, Babe Didrikson, perhaps the twentieth century's most gifted all-around athlete, won three medals in track events at the 1932 Olympics in Los Angeles and later dominated the women's professional golf tour.[24]

In general, American girls found lots of opportunities for vigorous exercise and play in both the nineteenth and twentieth centuries, either informally in their neighborhoods or through schools, YWCAs, or settlement houses. But especially after they reached adolescence, girls were often told to pin up their hair, lengthen their skirts, and start acting more conventionally feminine. The tension between athletic competition and femininity ("nice girls don't sweat") is one that continues to the present day, as manifested in the tendency for female athletes to try to conform as closely as possible to dominant cultural standards of beauty, behavior, and grooming. Such nods to conformity often also represent an attempt to distance women's sports from a longstanding—and misleading—association with lesbianism, which in turn increases the difficulty for women athletes who are lesbians to be comfortable and public about their sexual orientation.[25]

In addition to homophobia, women's sports have often divided along lines of class and race. In general, individual sports such as tennis, figure skating, and golf have had higher status and broader public approval than team sports such as basketball or softball; not coincidentally, those individual sports are more expensive to pursue and thus have been more available to elite, usually white, women. Conversely, working-class women have sought out opportunities to play recreational softball or basketball through industrial leagues or the American Athletic Union (AAU), which sponsors and organizes competitions for teams not linked to schools or universities. In the 1940s and 1950s, sports like track and field became the province of small black colleges and universities in the South, especially Tuskegee Institute and Tennessee State University (which produced sprinter Wilma Rudolph), in part because track and field was shunned by white female athletes.[26]

For many women, their formative athletic experiences occurred as part of their schooling, especially in physical education classes and intramural sports. Here they could not avoid confronting the fact that physical activity for girls occurred in a very different universe than similar activity for boys. Starting early in the twentieth century, female athletic leaders put forward a philosophy, carefully nurtured in schools and physical education departments across the country, that was summed up by the phrase "a sport for every girl and every girl in a sport." This model emphasized participation and play rather than the competition and winning that increasingly dominated athletics for men. Play days and other informal competitions were prized over varsity intercollegiate competition as opportunities to promote healthful exercise without compromising femininity. Chances for talented athletes to compete and win took a back seat to opening competition to all comers, no matter what their skill level. Other manifestations of this different approach to women's sports were special girls' rules for basketball (six players, no roving, limits on dribbling) and outright bans on contact sports like ice hockey and football.[27]

In retrospect, changes were already underway in women's sports in the decades before the passage of Title IX. One example was the expansion of women's participation in the Olympics—from 384 competitors in 1956 to 1,247 in 1976—fueled in part by Cold War rivalries with Soviet bloc states. If the United States was going to hold its own against Soviet athletes in the medal race, it needed the contributions of well-trained female athletes in addition to those of its men. A similar process opened opportunities for black athletes and indirectly helped weaken racial segregation in those years.[28]

Another example of change underway was the 1966 formation of the Commission on Intercollegiate Athletics for Women (CIAW). This group was created to encourage the expansion of opportunities for college women's athletics while also holding on to the more "woman-defined" approach of groups such as the National Section for Girls' and Women's Sports (its parent organization) and the National Association for the Physical Education of College Women. As part of its mandate to build a governance structure for women's intercollegiate athletics, CIAW began offering national championships in two sports, with four more quickly added.[29]

The Association for Intercollegiate Athletics for Women (AIAW), founded in late 1971 and operational the following year, grew out of CIAW's realization that women's intercollegiate athletics needed a permanent, national membership organization to coordinate its activities. Like its predecessors, the AIAW shared a commitment to a more participation-oriented, less elitist approach to sports that differed fundamentally from the reigning male model of sports which intertwined competition, winning, and commercialization. For example, determined not to simply ape men's sports, the AIAW initially banned the awarding of athletic scholarships. But the AIAW moved far beyond the play day approach and embraced varsity competition as a healthy component of women's sports. Although not officially affiliated with the emerging feminist movement, AIAW leaders were moving in the same general direction. According to historian Mary Jo Festle, the main thrust of the AIAW was "whatever the direction of women's intercollegiate sports, it was women who should determine it." Its membership grew quickly from 280 educational institutions in 1971–1972 to 659 just three years later.[30]

Up until the early 1970s, leaders in the field of women's physical education and sports had been basically on their own. Their programs were small, and nobody paid much attention to them. All that changed with the passage of Title IX and the dramatic growth spurt in women's sports. Now the National Collegiate Athletic Association began aggressively eyeing women's sports. Could the AIAW stand up to the NCAA, the most powerful organization dominating college sports, and keep control of women's sports in women's hands? That battle played itself out in Title IX's first decade.

Women's sports leaders had many reasons to be suspicious of the NCAA's newfound interest in women's sports programs in the 1970s. As Margot Polivy, the AIAW's lawyer, pointed out, "If the NCAA had started women's programs in the 1960s, there would not be an AIAW. But now they say, 'You built a nice house there. We think we'll move in.'"[31] From the start, the NCAA had actively and publicly opposed Title IX, trying first to exclude athletics from it altogether and then working to exempt revenue-producing sports like football. When the 1975 regulations were announced, a lawyer for the NCAA pronounced, "This may well signal the end of intercollegiate athletics as we have known them in recent decades."[32] No wonder female athletic leaders were leery of the NCAA, with the most outspoken critics noting that the money the NCAA had spent lobbying against Title IX over the years would have made a tidy down payment for women's sports programs in its member institutions.

Once it became clear that Title IX was not going away, the NCAA decided that at least it could try to harness women's sports, in part to make sure that there was no competition for its power and control over men's. To that end, the NCAA began to plan a series of national championships that competed with those offered by the AIAW, with the additional carrot that the NCAA provided the championships at no cost to participating schools, a perk that the cash-strapped AIAW could not match. By the 1981–1982 season, the NCAA had prevailed and the AIAW folded. A significant chance for a different kind of women's athletics—less commercial, more focused on education and participation, potentially less exploitative—had been lost.[33]

STALEMATE AND NEW CHALLENGES

The period from 1972 to 1981 witnessed dramatic growth in women's participation opportunities and the amount of money spent on women's athletic programs. Of course, when you start with practically nothing, increasing the share to 20 percent may mean going only, in the words of gender equity specialist Bernice Sandler, "from absolutely horrendous to only very bad."[34] The real question was what it would take to get that percentage up to 40 or 50 percent, much closer to parity. For a variety of historical, political, and legal reasons, little progress occurred in the 1980s, but in the 1990s there was another surge forward. And yet a new wave of controversy and contention built in that [*backlash*] decade about whether increased opportunities for women were coming at the expense of decreased opportunities for men.

Even without regulations in place or active enforcement on the part of the Office for Civil Rights in the Department of Education (which superseded HEW in 1979), Title IX was still a very handy tool in the fight for gender equity. The threat of enforcement, coupled with the possibility of loss of federal funds (a sanction that has never been invoked), could put pressure on administrators or school officials who feared the consequences of noncompliance. Donna Lopiano, a former athlete who ran the women's athletics program at the University of Texas in the 1970s and 1980s, put it this way in 1984: "It was more like a guillotine in a courtyard. People were afraid of it."[35] The law also offered administrators a cover: When confronted about making hard choices or decisions, they could say that they had no choice because it was the law. For their part, women athletes who were struggling for better playing conditions were emboldened to make demands because they knew that they had the federal government on their side, at least in theory. And women athletic administrators, some of whom had been initially lukewarm about the law, began to sense its power when they saw how angry it made the men.

Since so much progress occurred without active prosecution of the law, some critics have concluded that Title IX wasn't all that important, that many of these changes would have happened on their own (and, the argument goes on, would continue today without federal interference).[36] This line of reasoning is challenged by the concerted effort that administrators and the NCAA took in the 1970s to challenge or undermine the law's taking effect. It is also contradicted by the experience in the 1980s, when women's sports basically entered a period of stasis because the law was not being enforced.

The fate of Title IX has always been tied to the larger political climate. Its immediate passage in 1972 was heavily influenced by the [*context*] surge of legislative activism related to the increasingly loud demands of the modern feminist movement, which had its greatest impact in the first half of the 1970s. By 1975, however, when HEW was just

beginning to figure out how to implement this wide-ranging and potentially controversial law, the momentum of the women's movement had
stalled. A clear signal of this is the stalemate over the Equal Rights
Amendment. Only one state, Indiana, in 1977, ratified the ERA after its
flush of success from 1972 to 1974, and the amendment went down to
defeat in 1982.[37]

Given its long delay in issuing final guidelines for implementation, President Jimmy Carter's administration clearly did not consider
Title IX to be its highest priority. But at least the law was a better fit
with the Democratic Party's political philosophy than with that of the
Republicans who took over in 1981. As part of Ronald Reagan's
attempts to scale back big government and limit federal initiatives, his
administration promoted a general easing up on governmental regulation, especially in areas such as civil rights. These political developments, coupled with the concerted backlash against all the social
movements of the 1960s and 1970s, including the gains that feminism
had won, meant the early 1980s offered a chilly climate for Title IX
enforcement.

A more specific cause of the backsliding was a legal case decided
by the Supreme Court in 1984, *Grove City College v. Bell.* Grove City
College in Pennsylvania was an unusual school: It deliberately avoided
all federal aid to maintain its independence from governmental interference. Not surprisingly, with no direct federal dollars coming in, the
school did not feel that Title IX applied to it. In 1984, the Supreme
Court ruled that Grove City was in fact covered, because certain financial grants to students (indirect aid) triggered the connection. But in
what the *New York Times* called a clear example of "judicial activism,"
the justices significantly narrowed the coverage of the law from what
Congress had seemingly intended—that it apply to an entire institution, not just a specific program—by ruling that if Grove City were
ever found guilty of discrimination in a program not receiving federal
aid, Title IX and its sanctions did not cover that situation. Since no athletic departments received federal funds, suddenly they were not covered by the law.[38]

Any hope that institutions were moving toward gender equity out
of a sense of fairness and goodwill rather than fear of government
intervention or the loss of federal funds was quickly dispelled in
the aftermath of the *Grove City* decision, as schools cut recently
added women's athletic programs and scholarships and the Office for
Civil Rights cancelled twenty-three investigations. As Linda Jean Car-

penter and Vivian Acosta observed in a pointed understatement, "In general, the removal of Title IX jurisdiction revealed the ephemeral nature of the goodwill required for continued equitable treatment for female athletes."[39] After major increases in women's participation rates through 1981, there was no change at all from 1981 to 1985. Not until 1988, when Congress passed the Civil Rights Restoration Act over President Reagan's veto, was the broad coverage of Title IX restored.

Another pattern was clearly evident by the 1980s: a dramatic decline in the number and percentage of women coaches and administrators. In 1973, women had coached 92 percent of women's teams, but by 1984 this had dropped to 53.8 percent and by 2002 it was only 44 percent.[40] Even though there has been an increase in the absolute numbers of coaching opportunities because of the dramatic growth in women's teams, most of these new opportunities have gone to men. In 1973, women's sports had been run by physical education departments with low prestige and meager compensation. In part because of Title IX, jobs coaching women's teams became better compensated and more attractive to men; since the 1970s, the gap between men's and women's coaching salaries has widened, not shrunk, in large part because of skyrocketing salaries paid to high-profile football and basketball coaches.[41] A similar decline in positions for women administrators in athletic departments was also apparent. Although not mandated to do so by Title IX, most institutions merged the previously separate men's and women's athletic departments, invariably ending up with men in charge. This marginalization continues today. There are now far more women college presidents than women athletic directors, confirming that while Title IX had a significant impact on opportunities for student athletes, it did little to prevent backsliding for women coaches and administrators.[42]

A significant new chapter in the history of Title IX occurred in 1992, when the Supreme Court ruled in the case of *Franklin v. Gwinnett County Public Schools* that individuals were entitled to monetary damages, both compensatory and punitive, if their challenges were successful in the courts. (The case involved sexual harassment; Title IX prohibits discrimination in all areas of education, not just athletics.) Lawyers now had a stronger incentive to take on Title IX cases because they could potentially win big damage awards; conversely, institutions had a stronger incentive to settle cases rather than face long and expensive legal battles. From that point on, the trend was for lawsuits, rather than complaints to enforcement agencies such as the

Office for Civil Rights, to be the main avenue for raising and resolving Title IX disputes. As the stakes got higher, and resources in cash-strapped universities grew more limited, the level of acrimony surrounding implementation of the law increased dramatically.[43]

Ever since the original implementation guidelines were promulgated in the 1970s, athletic administrators and university officials have claimed that they were vague or unclear in their intent. In 1995, spurred in part by the 1994 electoral landslide that gave Republicans control of Congress, the House of Representatives held yet another round of legislative hearings to clarify Title IX enforcement; the following year the Office for Civil Rights issued yet another clarification about compliance. But was this ongoing foot-dragging really a question of the clarity of the regulations, or was it more fundamentally a disinclination on the part of university administrators to comply with the law at all? Most of the discontent surrounded the emphasis on proportionality as the main way to prove Title IX compliance.

Here, decisions made back in the 1970s came back to haunt administrators and athletic directors. When the regulations were originally drawn up, female undergraduates were in the clear minority, so linking participation opportunities to enrollments seemed like a good bet. In the intervening years, however, the proportion of women enrolled in college had increased dramatically and the proportion of men had declined, so that by the year 2000, women earned 57 percent of bachelor's degrees compared to men's 43 percent, practically the reverse from when Title IX passed.[44] Even if schools were working hard to increase opportunities for women, the gap was widening for reasons beyond athletic administrators' control: trends in higher education that were tilting college enrollments to a decidedly female majority. As Donna Lopiano realized in retrospect about the original compromise, "the shoe now pinches."[45]

Because schools had not always paid attention to the other modes of compliance besides proportionality, accommodating student interest and showing a history of expanding opportunities,[46] they were now stuck with the most difficult standard to meet. So what did institutions do? In the 1990s, many looked once again to the possibility of expanding new sports for women, something that had last been done on a concerted basis in the 1970s. In 1996, the NCAA drew up a list of "emerging sports," which put them on a fast track to having the minimum number of teams necessary for national varsity championships to be offered. Emerging sports included ice hockey, synchronized swimming, team handball, water polo, archery, badminton, bowling, squash, and equestrian.[47] Another fast growing sport was rowing (crew), which was one of the few women's sports that carried a large roster (as high as one hundred for the various boats) that could help offset football in the proportionality total. Another attraction of crew was that it was one of the few sports where an athlete with the right physique and attitude could be trained on the college level without earlier participation or training.[48]

While many welcomed these new opportunities for women's intercollegiate athletic participation, others rued that the very nature of the emerging sports might skew the racial proportion of female athletes to the disadvantage of women of color. "White-girl sports" such as golf, soccer, and lacrosse were much more likely to be played in suburban high schools or the private club circuit where white students predominated. Tina Sloan Green, director of the Black Women in Sport Foundation, said in 1999, "When you increase scholarships in these sports, you're not going to help people of color. But that's not in their line of interest. Title IX was for white women. I'm not going to say black women haven't benefited, but they have been left out."[49]

In addition to adding sports for women, some schools chose another route: cutting men's so-called minor (or Olympic) sports, especially wrestling and gymnastics, in the name of achieving gender parity. In some cases, men's programs were dropped in order to bring down the total number of male participants; in other cases, they were cut for budgetary reasons or lack of interest. According to the Office for Civil Rights of the Department of Education, which is charged with enforcing Title IX, cutting men's teams is a "disfavored" route to Title IX compliance. A lawyer who has studied the effects of Title IX agreed, calling the elimination of men's non-revenue sports "the least fair and least educationally sound means of resolving the dilemma of Title IX compliance."[50] Attorney Lynette Labinger, who won a major Title IX case against Brown University in the 1990s, made a similar plea for not simply cutting men's teams in order to comply with Title IX: "My mindset is preserve opportunities and increase them, not cut them in the name of paper compliance. That creates hard feelings and it causes people to assess blame, and that's always bad."[51]

Many commentators pointed out the insincerity of blaming cuts in men's programs on the need to comply with Title IX. After all, by the 1990s the law had been in effect for more than two decades and educational leaders and university heads could have been moving gradually into compliance over that period. Instead they stalled, or did as little as possible to comply. Now stronger demands for action were coming from a new generation of women athletes who were backed up by case law that made their challenges more likely to succeed. But universities were in difficult financial situations by then and did not have the resources to expand women's opportunities as easily as they did in the 1970s. Plus, women now made up a far greater proportion of undergraduates than before. Christine Grant, a longtime athletic administrator at the University of Iowa, faulted the leaders and CEOs of major institutions for dragging their feet over the years: "Through a proactive stance, the CEOs [could] have averted the current situation which now pits men's minor sports against women's sports—the have-nots against the have-nots—leaving intact enormous football and basketball expenditures and deficits. Blaming gender equity for the demise of men's minor sports is a red herring."[52] That is where things stood as Title IX entered the twenty-first century.

TOWARD GENDER EQUITY

What exactly is gender equity in sports? Here is how the NCAA defined it in its 1993 Gender Equity Report:

> At an institutional level, gender equity in intercollegiate athletics describes an environment in which fair and equitable distribution of overall athletics opportunities, benefits and resources is available to women and men and in which student-athletes, coaches and athletic administrators are not subject to gender-based discrimination.
>
> An athletics program can be considered gender equitable when the participants in both the men's and women's sports programs would accept as fair and equitable the overall program of the other gender.[53]

Minnesota gender activist Dorothy McIntyre offered a less abstract image: "When one piece of the pie is left in the pan and two kids both want a piece, give one the knife to cut it in half and the other one gets first choice. That's equity in a pie-shell."[54] A final definition puts it more colloquially: "If we are going to give jock straps out to the men, then we should provide [sports] bras for the women."[55]

The general concept of gender equity in sports enjoys wide popular support, and has since the 1970s. In a widely reported NBC News/ *Wall Street Journal* poll from 2000, 79 percent approved of Title IX; in a follow-up question, 76 percent approved of cutting back on men's athletic programs to ensure equivalent opportunities for women.[56] Polls as early as 1974 found that 88 percent supported equal funding for men's and women's sports. Note that these polls show the public is willing to take a far more radical approach to gender equity than most athletic and educational leaders, including equal (rather than proportional) funding and cutting men's sports.[57] It is probably easier to endorse those goals in the abstract than to have to find the way to make them happen. As the president of the University of Miami said in 1999, "I think almost everybody in higher education believes the goal of Title IX is worthy. The controversy is whether the end justifies the means, and that's the battleground where this is being fought."[58]

The root issues here are money and resources. As Alabama football coach Bear Bryant said in the early days of Title IX, "I'm all for women's athletics but if we had to split our budget, it would bankrupt us."[59] Even in flush times, postwar educational institutions have rarely been given a blank check to spend on either academic programs or athletics, and in times of recession and economic downturns, they face the same financial constraints as any business or profession. With finite resources and a federally mandated requirement for change, educational institutions have to make some hard choices.

Unfortunately, these choices are too often presented as a zero-sum game: If women win, men lose; if women's programs expand, men's must be cut back. Abundant evidence confirms that this is not necessarily the case: In the three decades of Title IX's existence, both men and women have increased their participation in intercollegiate athletics.[60] According to a study prepared by the General Accounting Office in 2001, the number of women's teams increased from 5,695 in 1981–1982 to 9,479 in 1998–1999; in the same period, men's teams rose slightly from 9,113 to 9,149.[61] Approximately 163,000 women participated in intercollegiate sports in 1998–1999, up from 90,000 women in 1981–1982; in those years, men's overall participation rose slightly from 220,000 to 232,000. Since 1992–1993, 963 schools have added teams, while 307 schools have discontinued them; most schools that added teams did so without cutting men's teams, although the largest Division I-A schools were the most likely to say that they made cuts in men's teams because of Title IX.[62] (See Figures 3 and 4.)

What these figures mean is that many institutions have been able to accommodate the interests and needs of an expanding pool of women athletes at the same time that they have maintained participation opportunities for men. They have accomplished this by reallocating internal resources, finding new sources of revenue, and trimming excess from bloated budgets. Walter Byers, the former executive director of the NCAA, put it this way: "The costs of Title IX and the

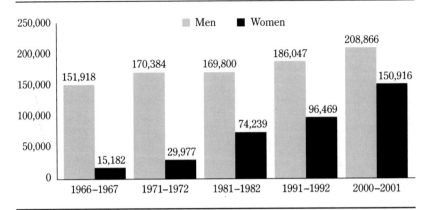

Figure 3. *Athletics Participation Totals—All Sports (NCAA)*

Source: NCAA Year-By-Year Sports Participation 1982–2001; Sports and Recreation Programs of Universities and Colleges 1957–82 (NCAA); U.S. Department of Education, Secretary's Commission for Opportunity in Athletics, *Open to All: Title IX at Thirty* (Washington, D.C.: U.S. Department of Education, 2003), 13.

entry of women into the big time should not be blamed for today's highly publicized financial problems for college sports. At the heart of the problem is an addiction to lavish spending."[63]

Nowhere is the addiction to lavish spending more evident than in football, which *Sports Illustrated* in 1995 called "that overfed sacred cow"[64] and Jessica Gavora tagged "the fat man tipping the canoe of Title IX."[65] From 1989 to 1993, the substantial increases in football budgets at Division I-A schools far outdistanced the additional money spent on women's sports.[66] A decade later, as the *Chronicle of Higher Education* reported in 2002, of 115 colleges with Division I-A football, 91 spent a larger proportion of their budgets on football than on all women's sports combined.[67] But try suggesting any changes to football coaches like Penn State's Joe Paterno: "Eighty-five scholarships is the bare minimum for football. I think if proponents of cutting football could come in and see a practice, they'd understand that.... People who keep saying we should cut football are on a course for self-destruction."[68]

In 1995, only partly in jest, *Sports Illustrated* posited three sexes when it came to sports: male, female, and football.[69] What has happened, especially since the 1990s, is that a rough hierarchy has shaped the context in which decisions about Title IX are made. At the very top are men's high-profile sports such as football and basketball,

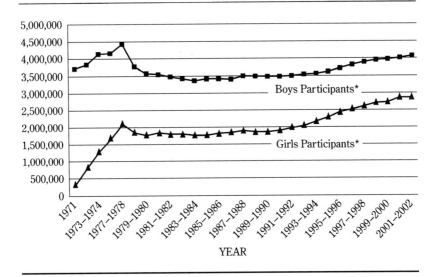

Figure 4. *Athletics Participation Totals—All Sports (National Federation of State High School Associations), 1971–2002*

*In years prior to 2000–2001, these figures did not include a portion of participants in combined sports.

Source: National Federation of State High School Associations 2002 Participation Survey; U.S. Department of Education, Secretary's Commission for Opportunity in Athletics, *Open to All: Title IX at Thirty* (Washington, D.C.: U.S. Department of Education, 2003), 14.

the budgets of which continue to expand and consume a large portion of the overall athletic budget and which, contrary to popular myths, do not necessarily bring in revenue. While women's sports activists repeatedly point out that money shaved from bloated football budgets would more than pay for women's sports, so far most football programs have proven immune to major cuts or changes. That leaves women's sports and all the remaining men's sports to fight it out for the remaining resources, with women's sports holding a slight edge (in large part because of the threat of Title IX litigation) and expensive men's sports such as gymnastics and wrestling being especially at risk.[70] Sports historian Mary Jo Kane called this "a very clever strategy to have men's minor sports being pitted against women," but she also noted, "The irony in all this is that if men's nonrevenue sports would team up with women's sports and go after football, [reducing] the size and expenditures in football, you could add sports for women and very comfortably support men's nonrevenue sports."[71] Donna

Lopiano put it well: "Football is pitting the victims against the victims. Until they rise up, men's minor sports will be crying the blues as football keeps laughing to the bank."[72]

The stakes in this battle over resources are especially high for women athletes, because in a classic case of "blaming the victim," too often women and Title IX, rather than decisions made by athletic or university administrators, are blamed for cuts and changes in men's sports. Swimmer and sports activist Donna de Varona noted, "To create trench warfare between men and women is terrible. If it happens, women will be blamed, and they don't have to be. . . . The idea is to comply without being retaliatory."[73]

De Varona's use of the metaphor of "trench warfare" is apt, because in the 1990s the debate over gender equity was increasingly framed in argumentative and combative terms such as "battle," "tug of war," or "fight." In part, this reflected the increasing tendency for Title IX disputes to end up in court, which demanded an adversarial stance pitting one set of facts and interpretations against a competing set, with no room for a middle ground. Such battles in the courtroom, plus press coverage on either side, encouraged a tendency toward overstatement, taking cases out of context, or exaggeration, all in the service of scoring a point.[74] More broadly, this polarized and dichotomous thinking seems to represent a hardening of attitudes on the part of the lawyers, administrators, and activists who are waging this fight. A willingness to compromise or work together in goodwill toward a mutually beneficial solution is increasingly rare in such "us versus them" discourse. And the biggest losers may be the students who want only a chance to compete.

Since the 1990s, the focus of the debate over Title IX enforcement has increasingly shifted from how to improve and expand opportunities for women to the fear that male athletes, especially in minor sports, would be harmed in the process. As Jessica Gavora argues, "a law designed to end discrimination against women is now causing discrimination against men."[75] Instead of sympathy for girls who needed a federal law merely to take the field, the public now feels concern for male wrestlers whose teams are being cut. This current chapter is taking place in an increasingly conservative social and political climate, especially since Republicans captured the White House in the 2000 election.

It has been especially easy to pitch this "men lose when women gain" mind-set when men's teams are cut solely to improve the proportionality ratio at a specific school, which deprives men of chances to play their sport and does nothing to change the number of sports opportunities for women. These cases, while rare, are often widely reported in the press as examples of the absurdities that compliance has caused. When male athletes have tried to use Title IX to protect them from what they see as discrimination based on sex behind these cuts, however, the courts have ruled that this protection only applies to the underrepresented sex, women. As the Office for Civil Rights has said on repeated occasions, capping men's participation opportunities or cutting men's teams outright are disfavored ways to achieve Title IX compliance, and women too often shoulder the blame for the results of those decisions.[76]

The way in which women are often blamed for bad outcomes suggests that despite all the miraculous changes in women's athletics in the last thirty years, there are still lingering resentments and unease about women's prominent new role in the athletic landscape. As one sports historian noted, "Instead of championing them, female student athletes are still viewed by a generation of male leaders as half-invited, troublesome, stepdaughters who are depleting men's resources."[77] Men's intercollegiate athletics evolved slowly and fitfully over a century, but women, this view goes, had their opportunities handed to them on a platter without earning their place on the playing field. "There's no question that it [women's sports] ran before it walked," observed Cornell's athletic director in 1978. "The men didn't have what the women have now in their early years."[78] Caught up in an increasingly commercialized intercollegiate athletic system, women's sports remain at a disadvantage. "For many," Kathryn Jay noted, "women did not deserve equal treatment—even if mandated by law—unless they could pack the stands with screaming fans, just like men."[79]

UNINTENDED CONSEQUENCES
AND UNFINISHED AGENDAS

Over the past thirty years, the history of Title IX has been fraught with unintended consequences. The first, of course, is that lawmakers framed the law as a general tool to challenge sex discrimination in educational institutions without fully grasping what a revolutionary— and controversial—impact it would have on the field of athletics.

Another is the long-term negative impact on the employment opportunities of women coaches and administrators, who have seen their percentages plummet as women's participation soars. Also, there are the lingering questions about whether many of these changes would have happened even without Title IX because of the broad rethinking of the role of women in modern American life, including athletics, that has occurred independently since the 1970s.

Another unintended consequence of Title IX is that women athletes now often take access to sports, including the growth of professional leagues in fields such as basketball, volleyball, tennis, and golf, for granted. Girls and women in high school and college today have lived their whole lives in a post–Title IX land of opportunities, a huge difference from women just twenty years their seniors. Judith Sweet, past president of the NCAA, captured this well in 1993: "I never had the opportunity to be a varsity athlete, and when I talk to the female athletes and try to put that in perspective compared to the opportunities they have now, all I get are blank stares. That's positive because they can't relate to what I'm saying."[80] It's also negative, however, because it means that female athletes today have no idea of how recent and contested the access they take for granted is.

There are other downsides to women's increased athletic participation, such as the sexual abuse of female athletes by male coaches and the widespread incidence of eating disorders among girls and women who participate in sports. Basketball star Mariah Burton Nelson and runner (and later competitive bodybuilder) Leslie Heywood are among the former athletes who have come forward with their own stories of sexual abuse by their coaches, abuse rooted in the power imbalance between omniscient and powerful coaches and their subservient but grateful charges.[81] The desire for control and perfection that drives athletic excellence can also lead to anorexia and bulimia as athletes succumb to societal and coaching pressures to lose weight to improve their athletic performance. This pressure is especially severe in sports such as gymnastics and figure skating, but also affects cross-country, swimming, and others. (Male athletes face these pressures too, especially in gymnastics and wrestling.) So widespread is this phenomenon that the term "female athlete triad" was coined to describe how eating disorders and compulsive exercise can lead to muscle depletion and bone loss, as well as amenorrhea (cessation of menstruation), making women athletes more prone to injury as well as stress-induced immune disorders.[82]

Do women enjoy more equitable access to sports than they did thirty years ago? The answer is yes, absolutely. Have they reached athletic parity with men? Definitely not. Even the weight that should be given to these statements is open to conflicting interpretations. Activists survey the field and note that men's programs still receive almost two dollars for every dollar that goes to women's programs. As Congresswoman Cardiss Collins noted, "If schools designated two-thirds of their academic scholarships for men, we would be outraged. We should have similar outrage with respect to sports."[83] Not everyone, however, shares her outrage. Many who have witnessed the massive increases in the numbers and prestige of women's programs think that maybe it is time to slow down and put the focus back on men. Part of the challenge of studying Title IX historically is to try to reach an assessment of what has been accomplished and at what cost, and where the field of sports might go in the future.

One thing that is clear from the history of Title IX is that as women's programs have expanded and solidified their place in the academy, they have not caused a fundamental value shift or reorientation in the meaning of college sports. Instead of being seen as a chance to find alternative ways to achieve both equality and difference, "Title IX came to be interpreted as requiring 'sameness,' and the model adopted was the men's, not the women's," Mary Jo Festle noted.[84] Another historian concluded, perhaps a bit too harshly, "In effect, as a result of Title IX, college sport acquired a women's wing, nothing more."[85]

The story of women's basketball is instructive. In the 1950s and 1960s, the top women's basketball teams were small schools such as West Chester State University and Immaculata College. Girls who loved basketball went to those schools because they knew the schools had strong programs; they weren't recruited, they didn't get scholarships, and they didn't play in fancy gymnasiums. (At Immaculata, a Catholic school in Pennsylvania, the nuns banged buckets in the stands to cheer the players on.) In the wake of Title IX, and especially with the advent of scholarships for women athletes, large universities with strong men's teams and big budgets could decide to attract and build comparable women's programs from scratch. Why would a girl join the Mighty Macs of Immaculata if she could get a scholarship (and television exposure) at the University of Connecticut? Small schools could no longer compete in the big leagues and quickly faded from national view.[86]

The growth of women's basketball is symptomatic of many of the changes that are reshaping college athletics in general as it continues to become increasingly commercialized and specialized. Standards of performance have risen so high that there is little room for late bloomers or walk-ons: Intercollegiate athletes in most sports have already been playing for years, nurtured not just in high schools but also in youth leagues, in summer camps, and even through private coaching. Multi-sport athletes are increasingly rare. Athletes are recruited for what they can add to a team, so they receive a definite edge over other students in admissions despite lower SATs, and their education often takes a back seat to their athletic performance. Graduation rates are dropping, and the exploitation of athletes is increasing. Television rights, game receipts, and winning seasons fill university coffers and put enormous pressure on coaches and teams to win.[87] These factors used to apply only to elite male athletes and coaches. Now they increasingly apply to women as well.

Does it have to be this way? The pre–Title IX history of women's sports offers an alternative model of sports that is more about the benefits of participation and the sheer fun of playing the game. As a former president of the AIAW put it, "Must the woman's rights movement demand for our young girls a share in the things that are wrong in sports today as well as a share in the rights in order fully to prove equality?"[88] Christine Grant also talks about some of these unintended consequences: "None of us wants to take away from the idea of gender equity in any way, but as it now stands, as we move more and more toward equitable treatment for men and women, we move more and more into creating the same kind of environment in terms of pressure to win, to get bonuses, to get recruits, to get fans, to get on television. We have to decide if that's the kind of success for women's sports that we want."[89]

Because the financial resources of modern educational institutions are increasingly stretched, some believe Title IX has the potential to reform and reshape collegiate athletics by causing a halt to the "arms race" that has caused athletic budgets to escalate in an unending quest for national prominence as the main measure of an educational institution's public value. The conclusions of the Carnegie Commission Report investigating intercollegiate athletics are even more relevant today than they were when the report was originally published in 1929: "The defects of American college athletics are two: commercialism, and a negligent attitude toward the educational opportunity for which college exists."[90] In 1998, Allen Sack and Ellen Staurowsky surveyed the defects of a collegiate system running amok and concluded, "Title IX and the struggle for gender equity have a greater potential for restoring the educational integrity of college sport than any reform passed by the NCAA in the past 100 years."[91] Restoring a measure of sanity regarding the role of athletics on campus and refocusing the student athlete experience more on education could be some of the most lasting long-term changes to come out of Title IX, although there is as yet little evidence that this is happening.

Someone once called Title IX "the biggest thing to happen to sports since the invention of the whistle."[92] It has been around for thirty-plus years and counting, and shows no sign of going away. Nor will the changes that have occurred in women's participation opportunities in sport: They have meant too much to individual girls and women and have been absorbed too deeply into the fabric of modern American life. The women's sports revolution is here to stay. Merrily Dean Baker, Princeton's first female athlete director, captured it perfectly: "I was called a tomboy, my daughters are called athletes."[93] Title IX played a fundamental role in that transformation.

NOTES

[1] Project on the Status and Education of Women, *What Constitutes Equality for Women in Sport?* (Washington, D.C.: Association of American Colleges, 1974), 7, 8, 16.

[2] National Coalition for Women and Girls in Education, "Title IX at 30: Report Card on Gender Equity" (Washington, D.C.: National Coalition for Women and Girls in Education, 2002), 14, 15.

[3] Kathryn Jay, *More Than Just a Game: Sports in American Life since 1945* (New York: Columbia University Press, 2004), 162.

[4] Gwendolyn Gregory quoted in Edward B. Fiske, "Congress Moves to Modify Law Restricting Sex Bias by Schools," *New York Times*, November 25, 1974, 23. For background on the passage of the law, see Karen Blumenthal, *Let Me Play: The Story of Title IX* (New York: Atheneum Books for Young Readers, 2005), and Welch Suggs, *A Place on the Team: The Triumph and Tragedy of Title IX* (Princeton, N.J.: Princeton University Press, 2005). See also Document 1.

[5] Quoted in Brian L. Porto, *A New Season: Using Title IX to Reform College Sports* (Westport, Conn.: Praeger, 2003), 144.

[6] Quoted in Mary Jo Festle, *Playing Nice: Politics and Apologies in Women's Sports* (New York: Columbia University Press, 1996), 112.

[7] Nixon signed the law just one week after the burglary at the Watergate apartment complex, the coverup of which would end his presidency two years later. The passage of Title IX was not the only event that month that would have major historical consequences.

[8] *Hearing before the Special Subcommittee on Education of the Committee on Education and Labor*, House of Representatives, 92nd Cong., 1st sess. (March 1971), 579–80.

[9] Jay, *More Than Just a Game*, 165.

[10] While Title IX applies to all educational institutions receiving federal aid, the focus of this introduction is on the impact of Title IX on intercollegiate athletics.

[11]"H.E.W. Head Says Title IX Won't 'Bankrupt' Schools," *New York Times,* June 27, 1975, 15.

[12]Linda Jean Carpenter and R. Vivian Acosta, *Title IX* (Champaign, Ill.: Human Kinetics, 2005), 31.

[13]"Prohibition of Sex Discrimination, 1975," *Hearings before the Subcommittee on Education of the Committee on Labor and Public Welfare,* Senate, 94th Cong., 1st sess. (September 16 and 18, 1975), 15.

[14]Candace Lyle Hogan, "Football Is Hardly Sugar Daddy," *New York Times,* December 10, 1978, 52.

[15]See *Favia v. Indiana University of Pennsylvania,* 812 F. Supp. 578 (1993).

[16]See Document 10.

[17]U.S. Department of Education, Secretary's Commission for Opportunity in Athletics, *Open to All: Title IX at Thirty* (Washington, D.C.: U.S. Department of Education 2003), 2. See also Donna Lopiano to Howard McKeon, May 15, 1995, in "Hearing on Title IX of the Education Amendments of 1972," *Hearing before the Subcommittee on Postsecondary Education, Training, and Life-long Learning of the Committee on Economic and Educational Opportunities,* House of Representatives, 104th Cong., 1st sess. (May 9, 1995).

[18]Quoted in Jessica Gavora, *Tilting the Playing Field: Schools, Sports, Sex, and Title IX* (San Francisco: Encounter Books, 2002), 73.

[19]*Cohen v. Brown,* 101 F. 3rd 155 (1996), 66–67.

[20]Carpenter and Acosta, *Title IX,* 72.

[21]Candace Lyle Hogan, "Title IX: From Here to Equality," in D. Stanley Eitzen, *Sport in Contemporary Society: An Anthology* (New York: St. Martin's Press, 1977), 420. The article originally appeared in *WomenSports* 4 (September 1977).

[22]For the history of second-wave feminism, see Ruth Rosen, *The World Split Open: How the Modern Women's Movement Changed America* (New York: Viking, 2000), and Sara M. Evans, *Tidal Wave: How Women Changed America at Century's End* (New York: Free Press, 2003).

[23]Quoted in Project on the Status and Education of Women, *What Constitutes Equality for Women in Sport?* 2.

[24]The quote from Louisa May Alcott is found in Betsy C. Postow, ed., *Women, Philosophy, and Sport: A Collection of New Essays* (Metuchen, N.J.: The Scarecrow Press, 1983). For general background on the history of women in sport, see Susan K. Cahn, *Coming on Strong: Gender and Sexuality in Twentieth-Century Women's Sport* (New York: Free Press, 1994), and Lissa Smith, ed., *Nike Is a Goddess: The History of Women in Sports* (New York: Atlantic Monthly Press, 1998).

[25]The best introduction to the issue of homophobia and women's sports is Pat Griffin, *Strong Women, Deep Closets: Lesbians and Homophobia in Sport* (Champaign, Ill.: Human Kinetics, 1998).

[26]See Smith, *Nike Is a Goddess,* especially 14–19.

[27]Cahn, *Coming on Strong,* covers this period.

[28]Jay, *More Than Just a Game,* 48–60.

[29]Festle, *Playing Nice,* 98–101, 109–10. See also Ying Wushanley, *Playing Nice and Losing: The Struggle for Control of Women's Intercollegiate Athletics, 1960–2000* (Syracuse, N.Y.: Syracuse University Press, 2004), chap. 5.

[30]Festle, *Playing Nice,* 184, 171.

[31]Gordon S. White Jr., "Are Women's College Sports Units in Peril?" *New York Times,* May 6, 1980, C16.

[32]Gerald Eskenazi, "Title IX Rules Issued for Equality in Sports," *New York Times,* June 4, 1975, 29.

[33]The *New York Times* extensively covered the battle between the AIAW and the NCAA. The most detailed scholarly account is Wushanley, *Playing Nice and Losing.* See also Festle, *Playing Nice,* 199–216.

[34]Quoted in Jay, *More Than Just a Game,* 171.

[35] Quoted in George Veysey, "Help on Way for Title IX," *New York Times*, April 22, 1984, 53.

[36] A prime example is Gavora, *Tilting the Playing Field*.

[37] Evans, *Tidal Wave*, 61–97, 176–78.

[38] "Judicial Activism in Grove City," *New York Times*, March 3, 1984, 22.

[39] Carpenter and Acosta, *Title IX*, 121.

[40] Ibid., 179.

[41] Welch Suggs, "Uneven Progress for Women's Sports," *Chronicle of Higher Education*, April 7, 2000, A52.

[42] Carpenter and Acosta, *Title IX*, 173–76.

[43] Carpenter and Acosta, *Title IX*, see the Franklin case as so important that they divide their discussion of legal cases into pre- and post-Franklin chapters.

[44] U.S. Department of Education, *Open to All: Title IX at Thirty*, 2.

[45] Donna Lopiano to Representative Howard McKeon, May 15, 1995, found in "Hearing on Title IX of the Education Amendments of 1972" (1995). See also the letter from Bernice Sandler that appeared in the *Chronicle of Higher Education* on March 8, 2002.

[46] The University of Missouri at Columbia is an example of a school that complied with Title IX by the "interests and abilities" test (prong three) by offering all women's sports available in Missouri high schools, surveying regional competitions in the Midwest, and looking at levels of club and intramural participation. The school would not have passed under the proportionality prong because of its large football team, and it hadn't added any new women's teams since 1997 (prong two). Welch Suggs, "Proposals on Title IX Intensify the Debate over Gender Equity," *Chronicle of Higher Education*, February 14, 2003, 39.

[47] National Collegiate Athletic Association, *Achieving Gender Equity: A Basic Guide to Title IX and Gender Equity in Athletics for Colleges and Universities* (Indianapolis: National Collegiate Athletic Association, 2002), chap. 6.

[48] See the chapter by Anna Seaton Huntington on canoeing, kayaking, rowing, and sailing in Smith, *Nike Is a Goddess*. See also Paula D. Welch, *Silver Era, Golden Moments: A Celebration of Ivy League Women's Athletics* (Lanham, Md.: Madison Books, 1999).

[49] Quoted in Welch Suggs, "Title IX Has Done Little for Minority Female Athletes— Because of Socioeconomic and Cultural Factors, and Indifference," *Chronicle of Higher Education*, November 30, 2001, 35. See also Jim Naughton, "Title IX Poses a Particular Challenge at Predominantly Black Institutions; The High Percentage of Female Students Makes It Difficult to Meet 'Proportionality' Standard," *Chronicle of Higher Education*, February 20, 1998, A55.

[50] Porto, *A New Season*, 156.

[51] Quoted in Carpenter and Acosta, *Title IX*, 73.

[52] "Hearing on Title IX of the Education Amendments of 1972" (1995), 121.

[53] National Collegiate Athletic Association, *Final Report of the NCAA Gender-Equity Task Force* (Indianapolis: National Collegiate Athletic Association, 1993), 2. See Ellen J. Staurowsky, "Examining the Roots of a Gendered Division of Labor in Intercollegiate Athletics: Insights into the Gender Equity Debate," *Journal of Sport and Social Issues*, 19, no. 1 (February 1995), 28–44, for the compromises made to agree on that wording.

[54] David F. Salter, *Crashing the Old Boys' Network: The Tragedies and Triumphs of Girls and Women in Sports* (Westport, Conn.: Praeger, 1996), 38.

[55] Welch, *Silver Era, Golden Moments*, 57.

[56] Welch Suggs, "Poll Finds Strong Public Backing for Gender Equity in College Athletics," *Chronicle of Higher Education*, July 7, 2000, A40.

[57] Lee Sigelman and Clyde Wilcox, "Public Support for Gender Equity in Athletics Programs," *Women & Politics*, 22, no. 1 (2001), 85, 89.

[58] James C. Garland quoted in Welch Suggs, "Colleges Consider Fairness of Cutting Men's Teams to Comply with Title IX," *Chronicle of Higher Education*, February 19, 1999, A53.

[59] Quoted in Festle, *Playing Nice*, 127.

[60] See, for example, Peter L. Shaw, "Achieving Title IX Gender Equity in College Athletics in an Era of Fiscal Austerity," *Journal of Sport and Social Issues* 19, no. 1 (February 1995), 6–27, and Don Sabo, "Women's Athletics and the Elimination of Men's Sports Programs," *Journal of Sport and Social Issues*, 22, no. 1 (February 1998), 27–31.

[61] General Accounting Office, "Intercollegiate Athletics: Four-Year Colleges' Experiences Adding and Discontinuing Teams" (Washington, D.C.: General Accounting Office, March 8, 2001). This statistic is the source of the claim, often cited by opponents of further Title IX change, that women now have more teams than men and thus have made a major stride toward equality. When the numbers of actual participants on these teams are tallied, however, men still receive a substantial majority of participation opportunities because of football.

[62] GAO, "Intercollegiate Athletics." See also Jennifer Jacobson, "Colleges Cut Men's Teams," *Chronicle of Higher Education*, March 23, 2001, 44.

[63] Porto, *A New Season*, 61.

[64] Alexander Wolff and Richard O'Brien, "Scorecard," *Sports Illustrated*, February 6, 1995.

[65] Gavora was referring specifically to the large numbers of athletes involved, which make it difficult for any school with a large football program to achieve proportionality between male and female athletes. In other contexts, however, she is critical of how men's minor sports have been sacrificed in order to achieve compliance. *Tilting the Playing Field*, 60.

[66] Donald F. Mahony and Donna Pastore, "Distributive Justice: An Examination of Participation Opportunities, Revenues, and Expenses at NCAA Institutions, 1973–1993," *Journal of Sport and Social Issues*, 22, no. 2 (May 1998), 148.

[67] Welch Suggs, "Title IX at 30," *Chronicle of Higher Education*, June 21, 2002, 38.

[68] Joe Paterno quoted in Steve Wieberg, "Bid for Proportionality Has Its Costs," *USA Today*, June 20, 1997, 11C.

[69] Wolff and O'Brien, "Scorecard."

[70] According to Mahoney and Pastore, "Distributive Justice," over the period 1973–1993 the strategy seemed to be to take money from men's minor sports to give to women's sports, as reflected in a declining percentage of resources (42 percent in 1973 versus 28 percent in 1993) that men's minor sports commanded in the overall budget (148).

[71] Quoted in Gavora, *Tilting the Playing Field*, 63.

[72] Quoted in Porto, *A New Season*, 57.

[73] Quoted in Ellen J. Staurowsky, "Critiquing the Language of the Gender Equity Debate," *Journal of Sport and Social Issues*, 22, no. 1 (February 1998), 10.

[74] Staurowsky's "Critiquing the Language of the Gender Equity Debate" is excellent on this point. While some of the most outrageous overstatements have come from football coaches predicting disaster if football is touched, Staurowsky points out that activists like the Women's Sports Foundation also engage in hyperbole and overstatement. One example she cites is the repeated references to how sports are good for girls and women in terms of lowering the risk of breast cancer, building self-esteem, and ending spousal abuse. Boys and men are never expected to justify why sports are good for them: It's a given.

[75] Gavora, *Tilting the Playing Field*, 4. See also Leo Kocher, "1972: 'You Can't Play Because You're a Girl'; 2004: 'You Can't Play Because You're a Boy,'" in Rita J. Simon, ed., *Sporting Equality: Title IX Thirty Years Later* (New Brunswick, N.J.: Transaction Publishers, 2005), 147–63.

[76] See the statement of Norma Cantu, head of the Office of Civil Rights, in "Hearing on Title IX of the Education Amendments of 1972" (1995).

[77] Festle, *Playing Nice*, 280.

[78] "Cornell Unable to Meet Sports Proportionality Deadline," *New York Times*, March 4, 1978, 16.

[79]Jay, *More Than Just a Game*, 241.

[80]Carpenter and Acosta, *Title IX*, 109.

[81]See Leslie Heywood, *Pretty Good for a Girl: An Athlete's Story* (New York: Free Press, 1998), and Mariah Burton Nelson, *The Stronger Women Get, The More Men Love Football: Sexism and the American Culture of Sports* (New York: Harcourt Brace, 1994).

[82]Heywood, *Pretty Good for a Girl*, describes how she pushed her body so far when running track that she developed mixed connective tissue disease. For another view of the problem, see Merrell Noden, "Dying to Win," *Sports Illustrated* (August 8, 1994), 54–60.

[83]Festle, *Playing Nice*, 279.

[84]*Ibid.*, 226.

[85]Staurowsky, "Critiquing the Language of the Gender Equity Debate," 21.

[86]Robin Herman, "Women's Basketball Arrives," *New York Times*, March 20, 1978, C1. For more on women and basketball, see Pamela Grundy and Susan Shackelford, *Shattering the Glass: The Remarkable History of Women's Basketball* (New York: The New Press, 2005), and Julie Byrne, *O God of Players: The Story of the Immaculata Mighty Macs* (New York: Columbia University Press, 2003).

[87]For a wide-ranging discussion of college athletics that pays equal attention to men's and women's sports while documenting their convergence toward the male model, see James L. Shulman and William G. Bowen, *The Game of Life: College Sports and Educational Values* (Princeton: Princeton University Press, 2001); its empirical findings are included in Document 20. For the history of men's sports, see Randy Roberts and James Olson, *Winning Is the Only Thing: Sports in America since 1945* (Baltimore: Johns Hopkins University Press, 1989); Jay, *More Than Just a Game*; and Porto, *A New Season*, chap. 2.

[88]Shulman and Bowen, *The Game of Life*, 125.

[89]Quoted in Festle, *Playing Nice*, 281.

[90]Quoted in Shulman and Bowen, *The Game of Life*, 268.

[91]Allen L. Sack and Ellen J. Staurowsky, *College Athletes for Hire: The Evolution and Legacy of the NCAA's Amateur Myth* (Westport, Conn.: Praeger, 1998), xiii.

[92]Quoted in Festle, *Playing Nice*, 113.

[93]Quoted in Welch, *Silver Era, Golden Moments*, 156.

PART TWO

The Documents

The Back Story

1

BERNICE R. SANDLER

"Too Strong for a Woman"— The Five Words That Created Title IX

1997

While Title IX is today most commonly associated with athletics, the original impetus behind the legislation was the more general issue of sex discrimination in higher education. In 1969, women such as Bernice R. Sandler, who had just finished her doctorate at the University of Maryland, faced major hurdles in securing jobs or other professional opportunities solely because of their sex. Instead of accepting this as the way things were, she turned to the legislative system for redress. Her account of the events leading to the passage of Title IX in 1972 shows how a small number of individuals and organizations, backed by a strong ally in Congress (in this case, Representative Edith Green of Oregon), can almost single-handedly bring about major social change. In turn, Bernice Sandler's exposure to sex discrimination opened up a new career for her as an authority on women's educational equity.

The year was 1969. I had been teaching part-time at the University of Maryland for several years during the time I worked on my doctorate and shortly after I finished it. There were seven openings in the

Bernice R. Sandler, "'Too Strong for a Woman'—The Five Words That Created Title IX," in National Association for Women in Education newsletter, *About Women on Campus* (Spring 1997).

department and I had just asked a faculty member, a friend of mine, why I was not even considered for any of the openings. It was not my qualifications; they were excellent. "But let's face it," he said, "You come on too strong for a woman."

My reaction? I went home and cried. I had no idea that this rejection would not only change my life but would change the lives of millions of women and girls because it would lead ultimately to the passage of Title IX, the law that prohibits sex discrimination in educational institutions receiving federal dollars. Instead, I bemoaned the fact that I had spoken out at staff meetings with suggestions for improving procedures. I lamented the times that I had discussed teaching and professional issues with faculty members. I regretted my participation in classes as a graduate student. In short, I accepted the assessment that I was "too strong for a woman."

It was my then husband who helped me understand what the words "too strong for a woman" meant. He labeled the department's behavior as "sex discrimination"—a label that started me thinking. Was this really a question of my being "too strong"? After all there were many strong men in the department. Yet the label of "sex discrimination" was a new one for me and initially I was not ready to apply it to my not getting the position at Maryland. Like many women at that time, I was somewhat ambivalent about the women's movement and halfway believed the press descriptions of its supporters as "abrasive," "man-hating," "radical," and "unfeminine." Surely I was not like that.

In the next few months I had two more similar rejections. A research executive who interviewed me for a position spent nearly an hour explaining to me why he wouldn't hire women because they stayed at home when their children were sick. (That my children were in high school was deemed irrelevant.) Then an employment agency counselor looked at my resume and told me that I was "not really a professional" but "just a housewife who went back to school."

Although later, in retrospect, I would discover other instances of sex discrimination in my life, at that point I had not consciously noticed it. Yet here were three incidents within a short period which I could not rationalize away. I began to think about the ramifications of discrimination and the burgeoning women's movement and to explore how the law treated sex discrimination. Knowing that sex discrimination was immoral, I assumed it would also be illegal.

But this was 1969. Although sex discrimination was indeed illegal in certain circumstances, I quickly discovered that none of the laws prohibiting discrimination covered sex discrimination in education.

Title VII of the Civil Rights Act, which prohibited discrimination in employment on the basis of race, color, religion, national origin and sex, excluded "educational institutions in their educational activities," meaning faculty and administrators were exempt. Title VI of the same act prohibited discrimination on the basis of race, color and national origin in federally assisted programs, but did not cover sex discrimination. Thus students were not protected against sex discrimination. The Equal Pay Act prohibited discrimination in salaries on the basis of sex but exempted all professional and administrative employees, including faculty. The Fourteenth Amendment to the Constitution assures all persons "equal protection of the laws," but at that time no case concerning discrimination against women in education had ever been decided in favor of women by the Supreme Court.

I began to read more about the civil rights movement to see what African Americans had done to break down segregated school systems and employment discrimination, with the hope of learning what might be applicable to women's issues. The breakthrough occurred when I was reading a report of the U.S. Commission on Civil Rights which examined the impact of antidiscrimination laws on race discrimination. The report described a presidential Executive Order prohibiting federal contractors from discrimination in employment on the basis of race, color, religion and national origin. There was a footnote, and being an academic, I quickly turned to the back of the report to read it. It stated that Executive Order 11246 had been amended by President Johnson, effective October 13, 1968, to include discrimination based on sex.

Even though I was alone, I shrieked aloud with my discovery: I had made the connection that since most universities and colleges had federal contracts they were forbidden from discriminating in employment on the basis of sex. Yes, there was a legal route to combat sex discrimination even though few people knew it at the time.

I called the Office of Federal Contract Compliance at the Department of Labor to be certain that sex discrimination was covered by the Executive Order. I was immediately connected to the Director, Vincent Macaluso, who had been waiting for someone to use the Executive Order in regard to sex discrimination. We met, and together we planned the first complaint against universities and colleges, and the strategies to bring about enforcement of the Executive Order.

Two months later under the auspices of the Women's Equity Action League (WEAL) I began what was soon to become a national campaign to end discrimination in education and which eventually culminated in the passage of Title IX. On January 31, 1970 WEAL filed a historic class action complaint against all universities and colleges in the country with specific charges against the University of Maryland. The charges were filed with the U.S. Department of Labor under Executive Order 11246, as amended, and asked for an immediate compliance review of all institutions holding federal contracts. Because these were administrative charges filed with a federal agency rather than a lawsuit filed in court, it was not necessary for me to be an attorney. There were no special forms to fill out. Individuals did not need to be named; the charges were filed on behalf of all women in higher education. Thus, the complaint did not name me or describe the incident in which I was involved.

Until that time the Executive Order had been used almost exclusively in cases concerning blue-collar workers, and although the order had covered sex discrimination since October 1968, there had been virtually no enforcement by the government until WEAL began its campaign.

The WEAL complaint charged "an industry-wide pattern" of discrimination against women in the academic community and asked for an investigation in the following areas: admission quotas to undergraduate and graduate schools, financial assistance, hiring practices, promotions and salary differentials.

At Macaluso's advice, I put together about 80 pages of documentation to accompany the complaint. He pointed out that a large appendix to the complaint was important; even if no one read it, they would assume that the many pages confirmed the charges. I included some articles and the limited data available, including a study of women faculty at the University of Chicago written by Jo Freeman, then a graduate student in sociology; and a study of women faculty at Columbia University by the Columbia Women's Liberation group. I also included similar data I had gathered at the University of Maryland, posing as a researcher. I underlined key passages in the document with a thick pen to catch the attention of anyone leafing through the materials.

In those days Xerox machines were a rarity. With the help of a friend at the Ford Foundation, 200 copies of the 80-page complaint were photocopied and sent to the press and others. Macaluso had suggested that copies of the complaint and appendix also be sent to selected members of the Congress, along with a handwritten note requesting that they write the Secretary of Labor asking him to enforce his own regulations governing the Executive Order; investigate educational institutions holding federal contracts to ensure that there was no sex discrimination; and keep the member informed of the progress of the investigations. Within a few weeks more than 20 members of Congress had contacted the Secretary of Labor. . . .

On March 9, 1970, Rep. Martha Griffiths (MI), who was on WEAL's national advisory board, gave the first speech in the U.S. Congress on discrimination against women in education, based in large measure on the information I gave her. She criticized the government for not enforcing its own regulations with regard to sex discrimination in universities and colleges. Her speech, the barrage of Congressional letters to the Secretaries of Labor and Health, Education and Welfare and the numerous meetings women's organizations such as WEAL and NOW had with the Departments of Labor and HEW paid off. Three weeks later, the first contract compliance investigation began at Harvard University. In June 1970, the Department of Labor issued its long awaited Sex Discrimination Guidelines for federal contractors and HEW issued a memorandum to all field personnel to routinely include sex discrimination in all contract compliance investigations. HEW also hired its first female compliance investigator.

But something else was happening in the months following the initial complaints. Rep. Edith Green (OR) (also a member of WEAL's national advisory board) had long been aware of sex discrimination in higher education, and the lack of coverage by civil rights laws. As chair of the subcommittee that dealt with higher education, she was in a unique position to shape new legislation. She had been urged to hold hearings by Phineas Indritz (a Congressional staff member who "dabbled" in civil rights issues) but she was hesitant to do so because there was little data available and apparently no constituency whom she could count on to testify.

It was a time when there were virtually no books and only a few articles that addressed the issue of discrimination against women in education. No conferences had been held to examine the issue. There was little research or data, and barely a handful of unnoticed women's studies courses. There were no campus commissions on the status of women and only a few institutions had even begun to examine the status of women on their campus. Women's caucuses in the disciplinary organizations were just beginning to develop. The issue of sex discrimination in education was so new that I received many letters from women and men asking me if it was true that such discrimination existed, and if so, could I send them proof.

With all of the WEAL filings I sent to her, Rep. Green now had information about sex discrimination in higher education. Because I knew almost everyone who was actively working to end sex discrimination in education I was able to provide Rep. Green with a list of people who could testify and provide the information needed to justify new legislation to prohibit sex discrimination. She agreed to draft legislation and to hold hearings.

The first Congressional hearings on the education and employment of women were held by Rep. Green in June and July of 1970. This was the official beginning of the bill that eventually became Title IX. The original bill, part of a larger measure on higher education, proposed to amend Title VII of the Civil Rights Act to cover employees in educational institutions, Title VI to cover sex discrimination in federally assisted programs, and the Equal Pay Act to cover executives, administrators and professionals.

I supplied the names of women (and some men) who would be willing to testify as well as the names of relevant organizations. I also testified. Because the original bill covered employment in general, there was a wide array of testimony documenting discrimination in employment, the professions, civil service, want ads, and education. No one from the official world of higher education testified, although they were invited to do so. A representative of the American Council in Education told the subcommittee counsel, "There is no sex discrimination in higher education," and even if it did exist, it wasn't "a problem." Apparently, Rep. Green's bill was not seen as being of much interest to, or having any major implications for, educational institutions.

There were seven days of hearings. Except for Rep. Green, who was in attendance throughout the hearings, only a few subcommittee members made short token appearances. Federal officials testified that they supported the aim of the bill but not the bill "in its present form"—a euphemism for opposition. Women employed in educational institutions across the country testified in support of the bill and provided data. Rep. Shirley Chisholm (NY) (another WEAL national advisory board member) testified that during her entire political history, her sex had been "a far greater handicap than [her] skin pigmentation." Other African-American women and female members of the Congress also testified in support of the bill. Much of the testimony dealt with the employment of women both in and outside of higher education; there was some testimony (but not much) about women students, mainly focusing on admissions and counseling.

When the hearings were finished, I was asked by Rep. Green to join the subcommittee staff to put together the written record of the hearings. (Thus I became the first person ever appointed to the staff of a Congressional committee to work specifically in the area of women's rights.)

The seven days of hearings resulted in a two-volume set of nearly 1300 pages. Because at that time there was so little written about women in employment and education, I appended numerous documents. This appendix material, which represented a sizeable portion of the information on women available at the time, included 14 studies of women at colleges and universities. As a result, the hearing record became a solid source of information about women for some time to come.

Usually only a few hundred copies of hearings are printed but Rep. Green received permission to print 6000 copies. She sent a copy with a note to every member of the Congress. I drew up a list for her to send copies to prominent organizations and individuals in higher education, and the press. . . .

The bill was ably managed in the Senate by Senator Birch Bayh (IN) who was also a member of WEAL's national advisory board. A few people (very few) noticed that athletics might be affected by the bill, and so there was a discussion on the floor of the Senate about whether the bill required educational institutions to allow women to play on football teams. Having inserted that notion into the legislative history, higher education retreated, apparently unaware that Title IX would have a profound impact on athletics even if women were kept off football teams. . . .

As the bill drew close to passage, a group of women (including myself) who represented women's organizations met with Rep. Green to offer our lobbying services. She informed us that it would be better if we did not lobby because there was no opposition to the bill, and the less that people knew about the bill, the better its chances were for passage. We were skeptical, but she was absolutely right.

In the spring of 1972, two years after the hearings, a portion of Rep. Green's original bill became law when Title VII of the Civil Rights Act was amended by Congress in a separate action to cover all employees in educational institutions. Initially, Rep. Green had also initially sought to amend Title VI of the Civil Rights Act (prohibiting discrimination on the basis of race, color and national origin in all federally-funded activities) to include sex discrimination. However, at the urging of African-American leaders and others, who were worried that opening Title VI for amendment could weaken its coverage, she proposed a separate and new title, which became Title IX. In its final form, Title IX was identical to that of Title VI, except that it was restricted to educational activities, contained additional exemptions and included the amendment to the Equal Pay Act. . . .

The historic passage of Title IX was hardly noticed. I remember one or two sentences in the Washington papers.

It would be another three years before the regulation for Title IX would be issued, and then another year before it would take effect. By then, higher education and the country understood that Title IX was going to change the landscape of higher education forever.

The entire WEAL campaign had cost a few hundred dollars in postage, but hours and hours of time from women in academe who patiently and painstakingly gathered and analyzed data about men and women in their institution, who pressed their Representatives and Senators for action, organized together and became advocates for change. They are the true unsung heroes of this story. They took enormous risks. Many did not have tenure and as a result of their activities never received it and were lost to the higher educational community. Some became lawyers or found other successful careers. A few went on welfare.

It was the words "too strong for a woman" that turned me into a feminist although I did not know it at the time. I have often wondered what would have happened if I had been considered for a position at Maryland. I might still be a part-time faculty member. Title IX, or something like it, would have eventually been enacted but probably in a weaker version with more exemptions, because of subsequent backlash.

For myself, I had no idea what I was getting into. I had no legal, political or organizing experience and had no idea that the political and legal action I began would force open the issue of sex discrimination on campus. I was extraordinarily naive; I believed that if we passed Title IX it would only take a year or two for all the inequities based on sex to be eliminated. After two years, I upped my estimate to five years, then to ten, then to twenty-five, until I finally realized that we were trying to change very strong patterns of behavior and belief, and that changes would take more than my lifetime to accomplish.

2

BIL GILBERT AND NANCY WILLIAMSON

Sport Is Unfair to Women

May 28, 1973

"Consciousness raising" was an important strategy of the emerging women's movement, and a three-part series in May and June 1973 in Sports Illustrated *helped to raise the nation's consciousness about the unequal treatment of women at all levels of sports in America. In addition to chronicling cases of gross inequity in terms of financing and facilities, the series examined the myths and stereotypes that held back women's participation. The final article, which took note of a possible revolution in American sports once women tired of being "programmed to be losers," was one of the earliest instances in the mainstream press to discuss the potential impact of Title IX on athletics, quoting HEW attorney Gwen Gregory as saying that guidelines for sports would be published in July. This goal, like many to come, was not met, but for those young girls (and their parents) who were tired of being told to sit on the sidelines, the knowledge that a new federal law mandated equitable treatment in athletics became an important spur to activism and social change.*

There may be worse (more socially serious) forms of prejudice in the United States, but there is no sharper example of discrimination today than that which operates against girls and women who take part in competitive sports, wish to take part, or might wish to if society did not scorn such endeavors. No matter what her age, education, race, talent, residence or riches, the female's right to play is severely restricted. The funds, facilities, coaching, rewards and honors allotted women are grossly inferior to those granted men. In many places absolutely no support is given to women's athletics, and females are barred by law, regulation, tradition or the hostility of males from sharing athletic resources and pleasures. A female who persists in her

Bil Gilbert and Nancy Williamson, "Sport Is Unfair to Women," *Sports Illustrated* (May 28, 1973), 88–91, 93, 98.

athletic interests, despite the handicaps and discouragements, is not likely to be congratulated on her sporting desire or grit. She is more apt to be subjected to social and psychological pressures, the effect of which is to cast doubt on her morals, sanity and womanhood.

As things stand, any female—the 11-year-old who is prohibited from being a Little League shortstop by Act of Congress; the coed basketball player who cannot practice in her university's multimillion-dollar gymnasium; the professional sportswoman who can earn only one-quarter what her male counterpart receives for trying to do the same work—has ample reasons for believing that the American system of athletics is sexist and hypocritical. There is a publicly announced, publicly supported notion that sports are good for people, that they develop better citizens, build vigorous minds and bodies and promote a better society. Yet when it comes to the practice of what is preached, females—half this country's population—find that this credo does not apply to them. Sports may be good for people, but they are considered a lot gooder for male people than for female people.

Opportunities for women are so limited that it is a cop-out to designate females as second-class citizens of the American sports world. "Most of us feel that being second-class citizens would be a great advance," says Doris Brown. A faculty member at Seattle Pacific College, Brown has devoted 15 years to becoming the best U.S. female distance runner. She has been on two Olympic teams, won six national and five world cross-country championships and set a variety of national and international records in distances from a mile up. Despite her talent and success she has had to pay for nearly all her training and, until recently, all her travel expenses. She was forced to resign from a job at a junior high school because the principal did not believe in women teachers devoting a lot of time to outside athletic participation. She has received far less recognition than male runners who cannot match her record of accomplishment. "Second-class citizenship sounds good," says Brown, "when you are accustomed to being regarded as fifth-class." This is not the whine of a disgruntled individual but an accurate description of the state of things in sports. To document the situation, consider the following:

Money Talks

• In 1969 a Syracuse, N.Y. school board budgeted $90,000 for extracurricular sports for boys; $200 was set aside for girls. In 1970 the board cut back on the athletic budget, trimming the boy's program to $87,000. Funds for the girls' interscholastic program were simply eliminated.

• New Brunswick (N.J.) Senior High School offered 10 sports for boys and three for girls in 1972, with the split in funds being $25,575 to $2,250 in favor of the boys. The boys' track team was allowed $3,700 last spring, while the girls' squad received $1,000. This might be considered a better-than-average division of money except that 70 New Brunswick students competed on the girls' team and only 20 on the boys'.

• The Fairfield area school district in rural south-central Pennsylvania is small: 800 students are enrolled from kindergarten through 12th grade. Nevertheless, in 1972–73 the school district budgeted $19,880 for interscholastic athletics. Of this $460 was actually spent on girls' sports, $300 of it on a "play day" in the area and $160 on a volleyball team which had a one-month season. Boys in the school district are introduced to competitive sport as early as the fifth grade with the organization of soccer and basketball teams that are coached by members of the high school athletic staff.

• In New York a woman officiating a girls' high school basketball game is paid $10.50, a man receives $21 for a boys' game. Throughout the country and with few exceptions, women who coach girls' sports in secondary schools receive between one-third and one-half the salary of men who coach comparable sports for boys. The woman coach often is expected to supervise candy sales, cooking contests and raffles to raise money to purchase the girls' uniforms and pay travel expenses.

There are many communities where tax-supported school systems offer absolutely no athletic programs for girls. In fact, until recently no money was spent for girls' interscholastic sports in two entire states— Utah and Nevada. . . .

Big Brother

• Dr. Katherine Ley, a full professor and chairman of the women's physical education department of the State University College of New York at Cortland, is one of the country's leading physical educators. She long has sought better opportunities for women in sports. At Dr. Ley's university (men's budget $84,000 a year; women's $18,000) the situation could hardly be described as one of sweetness, light and equality. For example, the Cortland women's basketball team cannot practice regularly in the main gymnasium, but it is permitted to play varsity games there. Recently one such game ran overtime whereupon, according to Dr. Ley, the men's basketball coach stormed into the gym and told the girls to get off the court because the boys had to practice. The women's coach asked if he couldn't use the field house, explaining that her team was in the middle of a game and had reserved the space. He said he was in a hurry because he had to leave shortly to scout another team. He told the women it was silly to finish; the score was lopsided and it was not even a game. The women docilely left the game unfinished and withdrew. . . .

If a talented woman withstands these pressures and decides to become a serious athlete, she often has to cope not just with insinuations but with a slanderous gossip. Jo Ann Prentice is a sharp-tongued, sharp-minded woman who has earned her living for 17 years on the LPGA tour. Asked about the "social" life on the tour, Prentice replied to the euphemistic question in her soft Alabama drawl, "This is kind of how it is. If you get into town at the beginning of the week and you meet some guy whose company you enjoy and have dinner with him once or twice, the gossips start asking what kind of tramps are these babes on the tour. If you stay at the motel where everybody else on the tour has checked in, then the question is what are those girls doing back in those rooms alone."

The vicious paradox that Prentice outlines—woman athletes are either heterosexual wantons or homosexual perverts or, simultaneously, both—is the culmination of all the jokes and warnings that began when an 11-year-old wanted to play sandlot football with her brothers and was teased, in good fun, about being a tomboy.

As a result, a great many girls simply avoid sports completely. Others try to compromise, accommodating their athletic desires to the attitudes of society. They continue to play games, but play them nervously and timidly, attempting to avoid appearances and enthusiasms that might be construed as unladylike.

The few women who survive the pressure may be scarred in various ways, but there are compensations. Jack Griffin, though he has worked for 25 years in relative obscurity, is regarded by many who know of him as one of the most distinguished athletic coaches in the nation. He has coached boys and girls, from grade-schoolers to postcollegians, in swimming, track, basketball and football. Working only with the youth of the small Maryland city, Frederick, he has helped to develop an inordinate number of national and international class athletes. He has been an Olympic coach and is currently a member of the Olympic Women's Track and Field Committee. "I enjoy coaching both sexes," says Griffin, "but strictly from a coaching standpoint, I have noted one important difference between them. Desire is an intangible quality which you like to see in any athlete. Coaches of men's teams often single out an individual athlete and say his most valuable characteristic is his desire. You seldom hear girls' coaches make this sort of comment. The reason, I think, is that *any* girl or woman who is very much involved in athletics tends to have an extraordinary amount of desire, not only to excel in her sport but to excel as a person. It is so common with the girls that we tend to overlook it, accepting it as normal. I suppose in a sense it is normal for them. The way things are in this country, any girl who perseveres in sport has to be not only an exceptional athlete but an exceptional human being."

The Early Years of Title IX

3

DEPARTMENT OF HEALTH, EDUCATION, AND WELFARE

*Draft Regulations for Interscholastic
and Intercollegiate Athletics*

June 20, 1974

Although Title IX was passed in June 1972, the Department of Health, Education, and Welfare took its time in developing guidelines and regulations for its implementation. Confronted by issues such as whether physical education classes should be coeducational and whether girls should be allowed to play contact sports alongside boys, HEW staffers began to realize what a complicated—and contentious—process this would be. Not until May 1974 did HEW circulate proposed regulations on athletics for public comment. These initial draft regulations contained provisions, such as the requirement of an annual survey of student interest and a call for "affirmative efforts" to publicize and create new opportunities for women, that were later dropped from the final version (see Document 4).

(a) General. No person shall, on the basis of sex, be excluded from participation in, be denied the benefits of, be treated differently from another person or otherwise be discriminated against in any physical education or athletic program operated by a recipient, and no recipient shall provide any physical education or athletic program separately on

Federal Register, Volume 39, Number 120 (June 20, 1974), 22236.

such basis; provided, however, that a recipient may operate or sponsor separate teams for members of each sex where selection for such teams is based upon competitive skill.

(b) Determination of student interest. A recipient which operates or sponsors athletics shall determine at least annually, using a method to be selected by the recipient which is acceptable to the director, in what sports members of each sex would desire to compete.

(c) Affirmative efforts. A recipient which operates or sponsors athletic activities shall, with regard to members of a sex for which athletic opportunities previously have been limited, make affirmative efforts to:

(1) inform members of such sex of the availability for them of athletic opportunities equal to those available for members of the other sex and of the nature of those opportunities, and

(2) provide support and training activities for members of such sex designed to improve and expand their capabilities and interests to participate in such opportunities.

(d) Equal opportunity. A recipient which operates or sponsors athletics shall make affirmative efforts to provide athletic opportunities in such sports and through such teams as will most effectively equalize such opportunities for members of both sexes, taking into consideration the determination made pursuant to paragraph (b).

(e) Separate teams. A recipient which operates or sponsors separate teams for members of each sex shall not discriminate on the basis of sex therein in the provision of necessary equipment or supplies for each team, or in any other manner.

Expenditures. Nothing in this section shall be interpreted to require equal aggregate expenditures for athletics for members of each sex.

4

DEPARTMENT OF HEALTH, EDUCATION, AND WELFARE

Regulations on Nondiscrimination on the Basis of Sex

June 4, 1975

In 1974 and 1975, HEW received almost ten thousand comments from the public about its proposed regulations on athletics. In response, the regulations underwent significant revisions. Whereas the draft regulations left the definition of equal opportunity vague, this new version identified specific areas such as practice times, coaching, and facilities for which schools needed to provide "equal athletic opportunity" for both sexes. (This original "laundry list" remains an important standard in determining whether an institution is in compliance with Title IX.) The regulations also made it clear that schools could not satisfy the law's intent simply by allowing women to try out for (and not make) men's teams, which would have barred all but the most athletically gifted female athletes from participating. Furthermore, the regulations set a timetable for compliance: one year for elementary schools, three years for high schools and colleges. After months of uncertainty and inaction, administrators who were eager to move forward with supplying equal athletic opportunity to women and girls breathed a sigh of relief; those who were content with the status quo worried about the changes the regulations might require.

§ 86.41 Athletics.

(a) *General.* No person shall, on the basis of sex, be excluded from participation in, be denied the benefits of, be treated differently from another person or otherwise be discriminated against in any interscholastic, intercollegiate, club or intramural athletics offered by recipient, and no recipient shall provide any such athletics separately on such basis.

Federal Register, Volume 40, Number 108 (June 4, 1975), 24142–43.

(b) *Separate teams.* Notwithstanding the requirements of paragraph (a) of this section, a recipient may operate or sponsor separate teams for members of each sex where selection for such teams is based upon competitive skill or the activity involved is a contact sport. However, where a recipient operates or sponsors a team in a particular sport for members of one sex but operates or sponsors no such team for members of the other sex, and athletic opportunities for members of that sex have previously been limited, members of the excluded sex must be allowed to try-out for the team offered unless the sport involved is a contact sport. For the purposes of this part, contact sports include boxing, wrestling, rugby, ice hockey, football, basketball and other sports the purpose of major activity of which involves bodily contact.

(c) *Equal opportunity.* A recipient which operates or sponsors interscholastic, intercollegiate, club or intramural athletics shall provide equal athletic opportunity for members of both sexes. In determining whether equal opportunities are available the Director will consider, among other factors:

(i) Whether the selection of sports and levels of competition effectively accommodate the interests and abilities of members of both sexes;

(ii) The provision of equipment and supplies;

(iii) Scheduling of games and practice time;

(iv) Travel and per diem allowance;

(v) Opportunity to receive coaching and academic tutoring;

(vi) Assignment and compensation of coaches and tutors;

(vii) Provision of locker rooms, practice and competitive facilities;

(viii) Provision of medical and training facilities and services;

(ix) Provision of housing and dining facilities and services;

(x) Publicity.

Unequal aggregate expenditures for members of each sex or unequal expenditures for male and female teams if a recipient operates or sponsors separate teams will not constitute noncompliance with this section, but the Director may consider the failure to provide necessary funds for teams for one sex in assessing equality of opportunity for members of each sex.

(d) *Adjustment period.* A recipient which operates or sponsors interscholastic, intercollegiate, club or intramural athletics at the elementary school level shall comply fully with this section as expeditiously as possible but in no event later than one year from the effective date of this regulation. A recipient which operates or sponsors interscholastic, intercollegiate, club or intramural athletics at the secondary or post-secondary school level shall comply fully with this section as expeditiously as possible but in no event later than three years from the effective date of this regulation.

5

U.S. SENATE

Hearings before the Subcommittee on Education of the Committee on Labor and Public Welfare

September 16 and 18, 1975

Two months after the HEW regulations went into effect in July 1975, Title IX faced a further challenge in the form of a bill (S. 2106), introduced by Senator John Tower of Texas, that would have exempted revenue-producing sports such as football and basketball from the law's coverage. (A similar bill had passed the Senate the year before, but had died in a Senate-House conference committee.) Senator Roman Hruska spoke in favor of the bill, and Senator Birch Bayh opposed it; Southern Methodist University student Nancy Kruh reminded legislators of the inequities the law was supposed to address. Over the years, all attempts to exempt revenue-producing sports from Title IX have been unsuccessful.

Statement of Senator Roman L. Hruska of Nebraska

My distinguished colleague and the author of S. 2106, the senior Senator from Texas, has made clear in his testimony that the extent and character of Title IX coverage of athletics is legally complex and subject to further judicial and legislative action. As he has emphasized, S. 2106 does not challenge the applicability of Title IX to intercollegiate athletics, although I have serious doubts about the intent of Congress in that regard. The bill seeks only the narrow purpose of excepting

---

Hearings before the Subcommittee on Education of the Committee on Labor and Public Welfare, Senate, 94th Cong., 1st sess. (September 16 and 18, 1975).

from Title IX regulation—before serious damage to the financial structure of intercollegiate athletics results—the revenues produced by and necessary to sustain individual sports.

Should S. 2106 become law, Title IX would continue to apply to all other aspects of intercollegiate athletics, including revenues in excess of those required to sustain revenue producing sports.

Mr. Chairman, I cannot emphasize too strongly the limited scope of this bill. The Subcommittee has followed a wise and proper course by limiting these hearings to the specific athletic revenue issue addressed by S. 2106. I hope that the other witnesses, the full Labor and Public Welfare Committee and the Senate will, if I may use an old saying, keep their eyes on the ball.

It would be most unfortunate if S. 2106 were perceived as a frontal assault on Title IX. It most certainly is not.

My able colleague from Texas has expressed his strong personal commitment to equality of opportunity. I fully share this commitment. But I also share his concern that such a commitment not be construed as any sort of acquiescence to massive disruptions of the affairs of educational institutions for reasons that go far beyond any reasonable construction and prudent enforcement of Title IX. Congress did not intend that. . . .

Now, Mr. Chairman, I would like to speak about this matter in terms more familiar to my constituents. Nebraska and its state university are typical of many Big Ten and Big Eight football participants. The University of Nebraska was chartered by the State Legislature in 1869, the same year that saw the transcontinental railroad link completed. This was two short years after Nebraska achieved statehood in 1867. The first classes at the University were held in 1871.

The University of Nebraska is a land-grant college with all that label implies in terms of large enrollments from within the state and the provision of many services to Nebraska agriculture and industry. Many members of the Nebraska State Legislature are alumni of the University. The Board of Regents must engage actively in extensive political negotiating with the legislature in carrying out its responsibilities. In the broadest sense, the University is a public institution and quite sensitive to the will of the voters. Its values and expectations have been shaped quite differently than those of many private higher education institutions, and certain public universities which were established much earlier in our nation's history.

Intercollegiate football emerged early as a major sport at the University of Nebraska. The name "Cornhuskers" dates to 1900. Down through the years legends of the skills and personalities of players and coaches, and the rivalries with traditional opponents, have been absorbed into the life and culture of the state.

For several weeks each fall in the wake of the busy harvest and on the threshold of our typically severe winter, the Cornhuskers unite the state.

Attendance at home games averages more than 76,000 persons in a state whose total population is just over 1.5 million. On a football Saturday the stadium is the third largest city in Nebraska after Omaha and Lincoln. Nebraska fans follow the team in large numbers around the nation. I confess to being one of the more ardent supporters. . . .

Last year the University of Nebraska football program generated an $800,000 net profit, which supported all other sports at the University. Major efforts are now underway to expand athletic opportunities in compliance with Title IX. The basic Title IX questions facing University officials are real, not academic. Will compliance with Title IX require the University of Nebraska football program to expand beyond its surpluses and channel sustaining funds into other sports? If so, where will the line be drawn? Indeed, how can such a line be drawn?

What will happen as the quality of the football program declines and revenues inevitably fall? Is the football program to be run into the ground to sustain other sports as long as it produces revenues, and then simply relegated to the minor sport category or abandoned? Or, will DHEW in its wisdom impose a revenue diversion scheme designed to assure a gradual rather than a precipitate decline in the quality of the football program?

These are the kinds of questions which cause University officials and the members of the Board of Regents to ask what are Congress and DHEW aiming at?

Set against these questions, S. 2106 is a reasonable measure for removing an awkward construction of Title IX. Its enactment into law would clear the way for Title IX compliance without unnecessary and confusing manipulations of football revenues at the University of Nebraska. The same relief would be afforded to other schools in a similar situation.

To the ordinary citizens of Nebraska, the apparent threat to the Cornhuskers posed by Title IX makes no sense at all. Why should an activity which carries the pride of the state be jeopardized and possibly sacrificed to achieve good purposes which common sense suggests could be achieved in other more direct ways.

Statement of Senator Birch Bayh of Indiana

The question before this subcommittee today is whether the Congress should retreat from the full commitment it has given to provide equal opportunity for women in athletics by exempting revenue producing sports from Title IX.

Mr. Chairman, it is interesting to me that in the midst of the highly vocal debate now going on over whether or not Title IX should apply to either revenue producing sports in particular, or intercollegiate athletics in general, no one is making the argument that there is not discrimination against women. No football coach or athletic director is denying that there is something fundamentally wrong with a college or university that relegates its female athletes to second rate facilities, second rate equipment, or second rate schedules, solely because they are women. No one seriously disputes the fact that athletic budgets for women are a fraction of those provided for the men. Instead, the argument has focused on the ability of certain intercollegiate sports to withstand the financial burdens imposed by the equal opportunity requirements of Title IX. To this end, those who feel such sports as football could not survive such financial strictures are seeking to exempt these sports from the mandates of Title IX through the Tower bill, S. 2106.

As the Senate author of Title IX, Mr. Chairman, I am opposed to the Tower bill, not because I am oblivious to the economic concerns of those members of the NCAA opposing Title IX, but because I think their concern is based upon a misunderstanding of both what is required under the Title IX regulations and the true implications of the Tower proposal.

What does Title IX require of colleges and universities in order to meet their equal opportunity guidelines in intercollegiate athletics?

Do the guidelines require equal aggregate expenditures for either male and female teams or individual male and female players? The answer is no.

Do the guidelines require equal separate facilities for any intercollegiate sports? Again, the answer is no.

Do the guidelines require that women be allowed to try out for contact sports such as football or basketball? The answer is no.

Do the guidelines require that equal athletic scholarships be given to male and female athletes? The answer is no.

Do the guidelines require that certain sports must be offered for women? Again, the answer is no.

What the guidelines do require is that when a college or university chooses to offer a particular sport to male athletes, it must provide equality of opportunity for women athletes. Under the guidelines, this equality of opportunity is provided in two ways. First, with regard to contact sports, the college or university may provide separate teams for males or females or may have a single team, composed of players from both sexes. If the college or university chooses to have separate teams, the institution is prohibited from discriminating on the basis of sex in providing the necessary supplies or equipment. Nowhere in the guidelines is there a requirement for equal aggregate expenditures.

I think one example of practice [f]or how Title IX would change things is that in one institution I know of for sport x, say basketball to be specific, if the men are trying out for the team, and the university feels that buying the shorts and the shirts and attendant equipment is a university expense, but the women, to try out for the women's team, must bear that expense themselves. Now, I think that is probably the best example that I can give you.

In a statement by the NCAA circulated among Members of the Congress prior to the congressional approval of the Title IX guidelines, the NCAA maintained:

> Throughout the entire, long debate over Title IX and the DHEW regulations, the NCAA members have consistently sought—not to have revenue-producing sports exempted from Title IX . . . but merely to make clear that revenues produced by a particular sport would be used to maintain the program in that sport. Excess of revenues over expenses in the sport would under the NCAA proposal be available for use throughout the intercollegiate program.

It seems clear to me that the NCAA was seeking an exemption which differs substantially from the Tower proposal in two significant ways. First, the Tower proposal addresses gross receipts and donations, not net profit, and second, the Tower proposal seeks a blanket exemption for any intercollegiate activity which provides gross receipts or donations to any institution for its support.

Under the Tower proposal, any institution's athletic programs could fall under the exemption of Title IX merely by charging a nominal fee at all intercollegiate activities which produce gross receipts or donations required by the institution for the support of that sport.

The original NCAA proposal states that the concern of the NCAA was not with a total exemption for revenue-producing sports, but with an exemption for moneys produced by that sport and necessary to cover the expenses of the sport.

In other words, the net profit of the sport, not its gross receipts or initial donations.

The Tower amendment does not provide a partial exemption [from] Title IX for revenue-producing sports, it provides a blanket exemption. The only criteria necessary to achieve the exemption is the production of revenues or donations. The specific wording of the Tower bill is not directed to the moneys necessary to cover expenses of a particular sport, rather it is directed at creating a total exemption for the sport itself from Title IX.

Therefore, despite the initial statement of the NCAA that the NCAA membership was not seeking such a blanket exemption from Title IX, this is exactly what is created by the Tower amendment, Mr. Chairman.

In conclusion, Mr. Chairman, let me say that from the college coed to the 10-year-old longing to play Little League baseball, American women have been consistently denied adequate athletic opportunities. Funding, coaching, scheduling, scholarships, and access to facilities are only a few of the areas where inequities are glaring.

Title IX attempts to address these inequities, not through rigid requirements of equal expenditures for males and females, but through an assessment of a variety of factors including student interest and participation, past history of athletic opportunities for members of both sexes, and current fiscal constraints that will vary from institution to institution.

For years women's intercollegiate athletics have had to struggle by with very little institutional assistance. For the first time, under Title IX, women athletes will be afforded a true opportunity to use their skills and aptitudes. I hope that members of this subcommittee will help make sure that after years of deprivation, support will be there for women's athletic programs throughout this Nation.

I am concerned, Mr. Chairman, that this subcommittee not begin the erosion of our commitment to the women of this Nation through Title IX. In this particular instance we are talking about our commitment to the women athletes throughout this Nation's colleges and universities, but once the Pandora's box of successful exemptions to Title IX is opened, we will see a host of other deserving exemptions being offered.

Therefore, Mr. Chairman, I urge you and other members of the subcommittee to reject the bill of our distinguished colleague from Texas and leave the congressional commitment to women through Title IX unscarred.

I might say, Mr. Chairman, I have had the opportunity, I suppose, as much as anybody in this body to study what we are trying to accomplish through Title IX. It is unbelievable to me that sports programs so steeped in tradition as most of our big ten schools are suddenly going to disintegrate or even be seriously damaged or even slightly damaged by permitting the women to attend these same fine institutions and have an equal opportunity to participate in athletic programs and programs of physical education.

Letter from Nancy D. Kruh

3130 Daniels #3
Dallas, Texas 75205
September 11, 1975

The Honorable Claiborne Pell
Member, U.S. Senate Labor and
 Public Welfare Committee
4230 Dirksen Senate Office Building
Washington, D.C. 20510

Dear Senator Pell:

I am a student at Southern Methodist University, Dallas, Texas, and I am deeply concerned about the action your committee will be taking on S2106 (the Tower bill). I write to not only urge you to defeat this bill in your committee, but to also share with you the conditions on my own college campus which relate to this legislation. I hope, in some way, they will give you further insight into your decision-making.

As you might know, my school is a member of one of the athletic strongholds in the country—the Southwest Conference. But, even though we have some of the finest coaching staffs, equipment and facilities in the United States, horrifying inequities still exist.

My school has two potentially outstanding women's teams. The tennis squad has placed in the top twenty in the nation the past two years; the swimming squad, finally organized in 1974, placed third in Texas this spring. Unfortunately, these statistics belie each of these teams' training conditions. That they hold these ranks is an indication of their dedication and drive.

The tennis team is allowed to practice only on the slick and hazardous intramural courts, being barred from the newer more expensive men's varsity courts. As intramural season begins at SMU, the women will be obliged to forfeit practice time to non-intercollegiate teams.

Although nationally ranked, this team was unable to participate in many important meets during the season because of lack of funding. Also, much of their equipment is purchased by the team members themselves. When injuries occurred on the team last season, they were allowed the services of an athletic trainer only at 8 a.m.

After its formal organization, our fledgling swimming team was allotted no pool time last semester. The men's coach refused to give it time, and (as one women's team member understood his decision) also "thought it ridiculous to even consider letting women practice with the men."

Instead, the team was required to enroll in a swimming class. So, it received only a little more than two hours practice time a week, and, in effect, had to pay for the right to be on the team with their tuition money.

Two dedicated women team members rose each morning to swim from 6 to 6:45 a.m., before two to three male swimmers "took over" the entire pool at 7 a.m.

Because of lack of funding, the women entered only two out-of-town meets. Warm-up outfits were begrudgingly provided by the men's coach for only one of these meets.

Needless to say, while these women struggle to enjoy the competition and physical fitness they desire, the men have been given the best of luxuries. They have their own athletic dorm, training table, coaches (who do not double as teachers) and ample expenses for out-of-town games and tournaments.

I personally would never hope to have the same benefits for the women that the men have now. Instead, I would like to see a merging of these two extremes—the wealth and the poverty—into a reasonable and equitable solution satisfying all.

I believe the present Title IX regulations begin to find such a solution. Any attempt to weaken these regulations in the area of athletics will only inflict further struggle and hardship on women—such as those at SMU—who sincerely want to participate in sports.

If passed, the Tower bill will be a signal to all potential and active women athletes that this country's elected representatives are opposed to equal opportunity in athletics.

I hope that those who testify before your committee will bring notice to the fact that this Tower bill is more dangerous than it might seem. It is open to many interpretations exclusively favorable to men's athletics, and terms included in the bill remain undefined.

In closing, I believe it is necessary to add that I do not participate on either of the women's teams and so I write to you with *no personal* gains in mind. I am a concerned student and citizen—hopeful that the women of this country will never have to lock another dream or goal away because a social custom, or more importantly, a law says, "No, you can't."

I feel it important to mention, too, that I attend school in the state of this bill's sponsor, Sen. John Tower. And I believe that it is essential that you hear from people in this state. I hope I am not wrong in saying that there are many others here who fail to share Mr. Tower's enthusiasm for this bill.

I request your careful attention to this letter and further request that you enter it into the formal record of the hearings on the Tower bill.

Sincerely,

Nancy D. Kruh

cc: Members of the U.S. Senate Labor and Public Welfare Committee

6

RALPH J. SABOCK

Football: It Pays the Bills, Son
October 5, 1975

As the 1975 hearings demonstrated, football loomed over discussions about the implementation of Title IX from the very start. Supporters claimed that football revenues paid the bills for everyone else and that forcing any changes would be, in an often repeated cliché, killing the goose that laid the golden eggs. Critics of inflated football budgets, usually the most expensive item in most schools' athletic budgets, claimed that monies should be spread more evenly for all sports, men's and women's. This tongue-in-cheek opinion piece was written by Ralph J. Sabock, an associate professor of physical education at Pennsylvania State Univer-

Ralph J. Sabock, "Football: It Pays the Bills, Son," *New York Times*, October 5, 1975, 216.

sity, who insisted that the coach in the article bore no resemblance to anyone he knew. Many of these same points regarding football are still being debated today.

Football is one of my favorite games. I was, in fact, a high school football coach for 15 years.

Recently, college coaches have been pleading their case before government committees, requesting reconsideration of the implementation of Title IX. Title IX is part of the Education Amendments Act of 1972 that means basically that equal opportunities shall be provided everyone in all federally funded institutions, especially public schools, colleges, and universities, in all phases of their programs, including athletics. Some football coaches contend this act will cause the death of college football because of all the financial ramifications.

It is true that the act was passed with little thought to guidelines and implementation, particularly in intercollegiate athletics. As a result, there is tremendous confusion.

Naturally, I was alarmed when I heard fellow coaches say that football was about to die. And since I was never a college football coach, I decided to talk with some coaches to find out how and why this insidious act could kill the sport so dear to millions of boys and young men who play it, the thousands who coach it and the zillions of grandstand quarterbacks like me who enjoy watching it.

Q. Coach, what do you see as the basic problem?

A. It is really very simple. If Title IX is enforced, we will have to share some of our money with the girls' athletic program. Since football pays all the bills, our program will suffer if they take some money away from us. If our program suffers we won't bring in as much in gate receipts and TV appearances, and as a result everyone will suffer. Therefore, football should be exempt from this act.

Q. Coach, isn't it possible to cut some expenses in a big-time football program and still not affect the quality of the game?

A. No way, son. You've got to spend money if you want great teams. You've got to go first class.

Q. Well, coach, why do you need 100 to 130 boys on a squad and 95 to 100 scholarships? Don't you only use 11 on the field at one time?

A. Depth, son, depth. You've got to have depth to play in the big time. Besides, we use two-platoon football. That makes 22 on the first team. If we go three deep that means we need a minimum of 66 players.

Q. Why do you give 100 scholarships when you might need only 66 players?

A. Hell, you aren't listening son. I told you we've got to have depth.

Q. Yes, but if you cut out 34 scholarships, that would save more than $130,000 a year, wouldn't it?

A. Yes, but some of these boys wouldn't be able to come to college otherwise because they couldn't afford it.

Q. Couldn't they borrow for a college education like most everyone else on campus?

A. Yeh, I guess so, but these guys have talent. And this is one way to recognize it.

Q. O.K. Well, what about training table? Why do your football players have to have special arrangements to eat?

A. Simple. We don't finish practice in time for them to eat with the rest of the student body.

Q. Why don't you shorten practice so they can get to meals on time? I understand this would save around $65,000 a year.

A. Yes, that's true, but we can't afford to shorten practice because it will hurt our program.

Q. Why must you practice as long as you do every day?

A. That's easy. Because all our opponents do.

Q. Is it also true that you take your entire squad off campus to a hotel or motel the night before home games? Eliminating this would save many thousands of dollars, wouldn't it?

A. Yes, but this keeps the boys away from the noisemakers on campus. This way, they can get a good night's sleep so they can play well the next day.

Q. Well, do the wrestlers, gymnasts and basketball players, for example, get to do the same thing?

A. Of course not, but our program pays the bills, remember?

Q. Oh, yes, I forgot. Well, how do you account for the fact that some large universities, most medium-size colleges and all small colleges have their football players stay on campus the night before a game and they still get their games played without any noticeable lack of enthusiasm and skill? Not to mention saving thousands of dollars.

A. I'll tell you, sport, that's one of the things that sets those of us in the big time apart from the others.

Q. How about spring practice? Wouldn't it save money if that were eliminated?

A. Yes, it would, but we've got to have it so we can experiment with the team to see what we want to do next fall.

Q. But if no one had spring practice you could do all that in preseason practice and no one would be at a disadvantage. Right?

A. Yes, but the quality of college football would suffer and the fans wouldn't come to the games anymore. We wouldn't make as much money and the whole program would suffer.

Q. But isn't it true that most football players dislike spring practice anyway, and if there were none they could go out for baseball, track and other spring sports?

A. Hell, boy, these kids aren't here to play silly games and enjoy themselves. They are here to play football, and we gonna win.

Q. I see. By the way, I notice that you have about 10 assistant coaches and about eight graduate assistants on your staff. Isn't 18 coaches an awfully large staff?

A. No sir. We've got to have that many to get the job done.

Q. Gee, if the average salary for assistant coaches were only $12,000 plus $1,000 for each graduate assistant that means the total salary for assistant football coaches is $128,000. Add to this about $35,000 for the head man, and it comes out to $163,000. That seems like a lot of money for one coaching staff.

A. Dammit, boy, you just don't listen. I told you before that it takes money to run a good program.

Q. Oh yes, I forgot. Sorry about that. But I did notice that some of the coaches coach only one position and have a total of about six or eight players to work with. I saw the girls' field hockey team practice the other day. They have one coach and 50 girls on the team. I don't understand that.

A. Well, that's what we call specialization. We can do a much better job of teaching this way. And remember. We pay the bills, and if we had fewer coaches our program would suffer. We would make less money and then everyone would suffer.

Q. Well, coach, I certainly can see that there is no possible way for you to trim your budget since there are no frills in your football program. It is also obvious that girls' athletics are a distinct threat to the future of football. First thing you know they'll want a new game ball every year and who knows what excesses in spending that will lead to.

A. Damm right, Ace. Let them share money with the wrestlers, track team, tennis team and those people. But leave us alone. After all, we pay the bills, and if we have to give up anything at all the quality of the football will suffer nationwide. The fans will not come to games anymore, we won't make as much money. . . .

7

MARGARET DUNKLE

Competitive Athletics:
In Search of Equal Opportunity
1976

The 1975 regulations gave high schools and colleges until July 21, 1978, to bring their athletic programs into compliance with the law, but institutions were expected to immediately survey their programs for potential compliance hurdles. To assist in this process, HEW contracted with Margaret Dunkle of the Resource Center on Sex Roles in Education to write a manual that offered specific guidelines for collecting and evaluating information about existing programs as well as suggested strategies for attaining equal opportunity. Complete with questionnaires and charts ready to be filled out, the manual looked at how the equal opportunity "laundry list" played out on a concrete, daily basis in terms of specific teams and situations.

Scheduling of Game and Practice Times, Season Length, and Number of Games

The Title IX regulation (in section 86.41(c)) lists the "scheduling of games and practice times" as a factor which the Director of HEW's Office for Civil rights "will consider" in determining whether or not an institution is providing female and male athletes with overall equal opportunity.

DISCUSSION

The lack of opportunity for women's teams to practice and compete can, perhaps more than other factors, dry up burgeoning interest in athletic competition by women. Often, women's teams have been "allowed" to use game and practice facilities only when the men's teams did not want to use them. For example, women's teams have often been scheduled to practice or compete at inconvenient times or off-

Margaret Dunkle, "Competitive Athletics: In Search of Equal Opportunity" (Washington, D.C.: U.S. Department of Health, Education, and Welfare, 1976), 35–39, 46–47.

hours in order to leave the most desirable facilities and times free for competition by men. Moreover, male teams have sometimes been permitted to have longer practice sessions or seasons at the expense of practice or competitive opportunities for the women's teams. Additionally, the process for scheduling games, as well as the degree of lead time in scheduling games, has often been quite different for women's and men's teams.

Because practice and competitive opportunities often differ so markedly for women and men, it is necessary to gather sport-by-sport information on scheduling, season length, etc. to determine if the overall opportunities for women and men are nondiscriminatory.

STRATEGIES FOR EQUAL OPPORTUNITY

In determining how to provide equal opportunity regarding scheduling, season length, etc. an institution might consider taking the following steps:

— Centralize the function of scheduling practice and competitive events and facilities in one institutional committee or office, taking care to assure that this committee is not discriminatory in its composition and orientation, and that nondiscrimination in scheduling is a clear mandate of the committee. Such a committee might either be composed of representatives from the women's and men's athletic programs, neutral third parties, or both.

— Reschedule events and facilities, so that women's teams and men's teams have equal opportunity for both the most "desirable" and "undesirable" times, etc. Note that "desirability" can depend on such factors as the day of the week, time of day, number of games, sequence of games, scheduling of "home" versus "away" games, conflicts with other institutional events, class scheduling, and the effects of the arrangements and timing on spectator interest.

— Schedule women's and men's games and practices in tandem or concurrently where possible. Note that care should be taken to assure that the practice times and places of women's teams are not dictated by the men's games and practices; such an effect could discriminate against the women's teams.

— Reschedule the availability of equipment, supplies, uniforms, equipment and training rooms, facilities, personnel, support services, etc. to assure nondiscrimination.

Travel and Per Diem Allowances

The Title IX regulation (in section 86.41(c)) lists "travel and per diem allowance" as one of the factors which the Director of HEW's Office for Civil Rights "will consider" in determining whether or not an institution is providing female and male athletes with overall equal opportunity.

DISCUSSION

Often the amount of travel, the mode of travel, the amount of money allocated for food and lodging, and the source of these funds have been strikingly different for women's and men's teams. For example, women's basketball teams have sometimes had to provide their own transportation and pay for their own meals when traveling, while their male counterparts have traveled first-class across the country at the institution's expense.

In determining whether or not it is providing equal opportunity in this area, an institution must first examine the per diem funds being allocated for meals and lodging to various female and male teams. Then, it is necessary to examine the travel patterns of different teams (i.e., the distances traveled and the number of trips) to determine if differential scheduling decisions are resulting in the provision of unequal opportunity on the basis of sex.

STRATEGIES FOR EQUAL OPPORTUNITY

In determining how best to provide equal opportunity in this area, an institution might consider the following options:

— Provide all athletes (both female and male) with identical per diem allowances, including the amounts allowed for lodging, meals, and other expenses.
— Schedule women's and men's games with the same institutions in tandem to the extent possible, so that travel costs are simultaneously shared and minimized. Note that care should be taken to assure that the competitive schedules of the women's teams are not dictated by the men's schedule; such an effect could discriminate against the women's teams.
— Institute procedures and specify a clear institutional policy to assure that college buses, cars, and other vehicles are equally available to women's and men's teams.
— To the extent possible, reschedule games of those teams which account for the majority of travel with schools which are closer.

Facilities: Locker Rooms, Practice and Competitive Facilities

The Title IX regulation (in section 86.41(c)) lists the "provision of locker rooms, practice and competitive facilities" as one of the factors which the Director of HEW's Office for Civil Rights "will consider" in determining whether or not an institution is providing female and male athletes with overall equal opportunity.

Additionally, the regulation (in section 86.33) provides the following regarding "comparable facilities" for women and men:

> A recipient [institution] may provide separate toilet, locker room, and shower facilities on the basis of sex, but such facilities provided for students of one sex shall be comparable to such facilities provided for students of the other sex.

DISCUSSION

Women athletes have often been treated as second-class citizens in terms of the facilities which the institution has provided to them. In the past it has been commonplace for the old gymnasium to be "retired" to the women when a new one became available to men and for women's teams to have fewer and less desirable competitive, practice, locker, and shower facilities. In some instances the lack of bathroom, shower, or locker facilities (or the lack of supervision in these facilities) has been used as a justification for denying women equal opportunity in athletics or in other areas. Although single-sex use of such facilities is permissible, it is not similarly permissible to use this lack of facilities as a justification for discrimination.

Under Title IX all facilities must generally be available without discrimination on the basis of sex. Locker rooms, toilets, showers, and other facilities available to women and men must be comparable. A close inspection of the facilities which women's and men's teams use, as well as a careful analysis of the access of each female and male team to various facilities and any related services, is necessary in order to assess whether or not there is discrimination in this area.

STRATEGIES FOR EQUAL OPPORTUNITY

If an institution finds sex bias in the provision of, or access to, sports facilities, it might consider the following alternatives:

— Develop a uniform institutional policy regarding the use of all sports facilities, making certain that both sexes have equal access to these facilities and are equally involved in making decisions regarding the use and scheduling of these facilities.

— Implement specific procedures to carry out this policy. For example, form an institutional sports facilities policy committee, with equal representation from the women's and men's athletic programs, to coordinate the use and scheduling of these facilities. Alternatively, this sports facilities policy committee might be composed of, or include, persons who are not directly connected with the conduct of athletics. Whatever the composition of this committee, care should be taken to assure that it does not permit sex discriminatory access to facilities.

— Remodel facilities, and/or extend partitions, curtains, dividers, etc., so that facilities can be used by either or both sexes.

— Reschedule the use of facilities so that both women and men use facilities at prime (and non-prime) times.

— Arrange locker room and other supervisory schedules so that students are not denied equal athletic opportunity because of less supervision or the unavailability of supervision. Implement alternative supervisory methods (e.g., using other employees or graduate or other students as supervisors) in the interim if there is the possibility that supervisory difficulties would limit athletic opportunities on the basis of sex.

8

JONI BARNETT AND THE YALE WOMEN'S CREW

Yale Women's Crew Strips in Title IX Protest
March 1976

In March 1976, members of the Yale women's crew staged a dramatic protest that drew national attention to the inequities facing women athletes and the potential of Title IX to change those conditions. Lacking access to shower facilities during their off-campus winter workouts, cold and sweaty members of the women's team waited on a bus for half an hour while the men's team showered in the boat house's only locker room before jointly returning to campus. Angered at Yale's slow response to their call for proper facilities and led by captain Chris Ernst, nineteen members of the crew team strode into the office of Joni Barnett, the director of women's athletics, and stripped off their sweats, their naked bodies revealing "Title IX" written on their backs and chests in blue magic marker. The story was picked up by the New York Times *and other newspapers around the country. The women's crew team got their showers.*

MARCH 3RD, 1976
Concerning Women's Crew Dressing Facilities at Derby Boat House:

A dramatic incident took place in my office Wednesday afternoon. Twenty or so members of the crew gathered to inform me of their frustration and disappointment with Yale's response to their need for dressing and shower facilities at Derby Boat House.

It is unfortunate that one of our finest, most dedicated teams has been so treated and alienated. Their resentment was such that they stripped off their practice uniforms and stood naked, wearing only "Title IX" in ink across their chest.

I have attached their statement to this note. I regret the women are not being adequately provided for, despite all of my efforts on their behalf. This project has been the #1 priority for the entire department

---

Memorandum of Yale Women's Crew to Joni Barnett, March 3, 1976, Records of the Athletic Director, 1970–1994, Yale University (RU 983), Manuscripts and Archives, Yale University Library.

for more than a year. I have urged action at every meeting in an effort to avoid the kind of image that has been created. This team has had my concern, efforts and interest. I sympathize with their anger.

It is not within my province to accomplish any more than I have already done. But I hope the University will react positively and with all haste. The solution, even a temporary one, must be accomplished.

The trailer has arrived at Derby and awaits the action of the zoning board of appeals on Tuesday evening March 9th. If approved for a temporary permit, it could be "hooked up" within one or two days.

I hope to communicate with you before the photo and article appears in the Yale Daily News. This appears to be news, since the New York Times had called within twenty minutes.

Sincerely,

Joni E. Barnett
Director/Women's Athletics
Physical Education
Yale University
JEB: jeb

Mrs. Barnett:

These are the bodies Yale is exploiting. We have come here today to make clear how unprotected we are, to show graphically what we are being exposed to. These are normal human bodies. On a day like today the rain freezes on our skin. Then we sit on a bus for half an hour as the ice melts into our sweats to meet the sweat that has soaked our clothes underneath. We sit for half an hour chilled . . . half a dozen of us are sick now, and in two days we will begin training twice a day, subjecting ourselves to this twice every day. No effective action has been taken and no matter what we hear, it doesn't make these bodies warmer, or dryer or less prone to sickness. We can't accept any excuses, nor can we trust to normal channels of complaint, since the need for lockers for the Women's Crew has existed since last spring. We are using you and your office because you are the symbol of Women's Athletics at Yale; we're using this method to express our urgency. We have taken this action absolutely without our coach's knowledge. He has done all he can to get us some relief, and none has come. He ordered the trailer when the plans for real facilities fell through, and he informed you four times of the need to get a variance to make it useable, but none was obtained. We fear retribution against him, but we are, as you can see, desperate. We are not just healthy young things in blue and white uniforms who perform feats of strength for Yale in the nice spring weather; we are not just statistics on your win column. We're human and being treated as less than such. There has been a lack of concern and competence on your part. Your only answer to us is the immediate provision of use of the trailer, however inadequate that may be.

—Yale Women's Crew 3/3/76

9

PROJECT ON EQUAL EDUCATION RIGHTS

Stalled at the Start: Government Action on Sex Bias in the Schools
1978

Having worked so hard behind the scenes for the law's passage and then having actively lobbied (not always successfully) to make sure its regulations were as strong as possible, women's organizations such as the Women's Equity Action League (WEAL) and the National Organization for Women (NOW) were heavily invested in Title IX's enforcement. In 1974, NOW's Legal Defense and Education Fund established the Project on Equal Education Rights (PEER) to monitor progress in the enforcement of federal laws against sex discrimination in schools. Frustrated by the inability of HEW to provide adequate documentation of its efforts or results, PEER began an analysis of every complaint regarding sex discrimination in elementary and secondary schools filed between June 23, 1972, and October 1, 1976. In addition to quantifying data such as type of complaint or length of time to resolution, PEER staff members also did selective follow-up interviews to see how well individual complaints had been handled. "Stalled at the Start," the report's title, foreshadows PEER's negative assessment of HEW's enforcement of Title IX.

Project on Equal Education Rights, "Stalled at the Start: Government Action on Sex Bias in the Schools" (Washington, D.C.: NOW Legal Defense and Education Fund, 1978), 7–8.

A ninth-grader in Livonia, Michigan, wanted to learn how to handle power tools, but shop classes were off limits for girls. "Women," she was told, "should stick to home ec." She wrote the government for help in 1973. Three years later, HEW wrote back, got no answer, and closed the case. The government never checked to find out if girls were still barred from taking shop.

"Something is wrong! I am doing more work for less pay," a New Jersey woman wrote HEW in September, 1973. She was coaching four girls' teams for one-third of what the school paid men to coach one team. HEW left her complaint in limbo for three years before closing it without an investigation.

Twenty-nine Minnesota school districts were discriminating against women in promotions to supervisory jobs, a women's organization told HEW in 1973. Of 152 administrators in those districts, two were women. Investigators did not begin to look into the charges until 1977.

These cases are not unusual. For half a decade, HEW's action to enhance equal opportunity in the schools has been negligible.

Title IX enforcement has been stalled from the start.

HEW brought relief to few of the citizens who asked for help in gaining equal treatment in their own schools.

— From June, 1972, to October, 1976, HEW managed to resolve just 179 complaints charging Title IX violations in elementary and secondary education — only one out of every five filed.

Most people who filed complaints met with long delays.

— Two- and three-year delays were not uncommon. More than a third of the complaints filed during 1973 were still unresolved three years later. The average wait on cases resolved by the end of our study had been 14 months. HEW intervention, when it came, tended to be too late to help the people who asked for it.

Most investigations were cursory.

— Most investigations consisted of little more than an exchange of correspondence with the school superintendent. HEW rarely talked to students or employees who might be the victims of discrimination. In 76 percent of cases where the government made a finding, HEW staff never visited the school district under investigation. As a result, the agency was likely to overlook all but the most obvious kinds of discrimination.

HEW has done almost nothing on Title IX besides its work on complaints.

—In more than four years, the agency completed independent checks on just 12 of the nation's 16,000 school districts. There was no follow-up on information it collected in several nation-wide surveys which showed likely Title IX violations.

HEW has had enough staff to enforce Title IX.

—From 1973 to 1976, HEW received fewer than two Title IX complaints against public schools each year for each investigator on the payroll. Out of those, the agency managed to resolve an average of three-tenths of one complaint per investigator. Even when the agency's other civil rights responsibilities are added in—complaints of bias based on race, ethnic origin and handicap—the total case load of complaints filed against public schools was just over six complaints per investigator each year. These people are fully qualified professionals earning an average of $20,000 a year. The agency should have been able to resolve all the complaints it received.

Indecision has been a major obstacle to action.

—HEW has failed to issue clear and consistent rulings on important issues it considers controversial. Rulings on some issues, such as athletics, have been deliberately ambiguous. Other rulings were reversed, or withdrawn when they became the center of controversy. For the ten months between August, 1976, and June, 1977, HEW stopped making decisions on Title IX almost completely. The agency did not even answer its mail. By June, 1977, more than 600 letters asking questions about the law's meaning were sitting in Washington, unanswered.

HEW's recent record is mixed.

—The record offers grounds for both encouragement and concern. Activity on Title IX has picked up, somewhat, since the fall of 1976. HEW closed more Title IX cases between October, 1976, and June, 1977, than in the previous nine-month period—192 compared to 122. In addition, since June of 1977, agency officials have sent out many of the letters on Title IX that had been accumulating in the Washington office since August, 1976.

On the other hand, the agency recently served notice that it does not intend to act promptly on most complaints. In its enforcement plan for this fiscal year, released in October, 1977, the civil rights office promised to investigate only 21 (7 percent) of the sex discrimination complaints the office expects to receive during the year. Agency leaders continue to delay making decisions which they think may stir up controversy. Dozens of cases are stalled awaiting rulings on those issues.

If government leaders want to enforce Title IX, the steps they will need to take are obvious. They will need to:

—publicize the law. Students and employees need to know how they can exercise their right to equal treatment;
—clarify the law's meaning on all questionable issues without delay, consistent with the principle of equal opportunity;
—make a commitment to resolve all complaints promptly;
—hold staff people at all levels accountable for the quality and quantity of their work;
—ensure that every investigation is thorough;
—provide adequate staff training and supervision.

Changes like these, however necessary, still come second. The first step is a decision, at the highest level, that the law against sex discrimination in education will be enforced.

10

DEPARTMENT OF HEALTH, EDUCATION, AND WELFARE

Policy Interpretation: Title IX and Intercollegiate Athletics

December 11, 1979

Even after the three-year transition period, questions still remained about what constituted compliance. HEW therefore issued this policy interpretation on December 11, 1979, to provide additional guidance. (It was designed for intercollegiate athletics, but HEW noted that the principles also applied to club, intramural, and interscholastic programs.) The major significance of this policy interpretation was the articulation of what came to be known as the "three-prong test." Under this test, an institution could be deemed in compliance with Title IX if it met any one of these three prongs. Not surprisingly, institutions, government investigators, and individual athletes often had different interpretations of how well a specific school was meeting the needs of women athletes, leading to further delays and more recrimination over the implementation of the law.

---

5. *Application of the Policy—Levels of Competition*

In effectively accommodating the interests and abilities of male and female athletes, institutions must provide both the opportunity for individuals of each sex to participate in intercollegiate competition, and for athletes of each sex to have competitive team schedules which equally reflect their abilities.

   a. Compliance will be assessed in any one of the following ways:

   (1) Whether intercollegiate level participation opportunities for male and female students are provided in numbers substantially proportionate to their respective enrollment; or

   (2) Where the members of one sex have been and are underrepresented among intercollegiate athletes, whether the institution can

---

Federal Register, Volume 44, Number 239 (December 11, 1979), 71417–18.

show a history and continuing practice of program expansion which is demonstrably responsive to the developing interest and abilities of the members of that sex; or

(3) Where the members of one sex are underrepresented among intercollegiate athletes, and the institution cannot show a continuing practice of program expansion such as that cited above, whether it can be demonstrated that the interests and abilities of the members of that sex have been fully and effectively accommodated by the present program.

b. Compliance with this provision of the regulation will also be assessed by examining the following:

(1) Whether the competitive schedules for men's and women's teams, on a program-wide basis, afford proportionally similar numbers of male and female athletes equivalently advanced competitive opportunities; or

(2) Whether the institution can demonstrate a history and continuing practice of upgrading the competitive opportunities available to the historically disadvantaged sex as warranted by developing abilities among the athletes of that sex.

c. Institutions are not required to upgrade teams to intercollegiate status or otherwise develop intercollegiate sports absent a reasonable expectation that intercollegiate competition in that sport will be available within the institution's normal competitive regions. Institutions may be required by the Title IX regulation to actively encourage the development of such competition, however, when overall athletic opportunities within that region have been historically limited for the members of one sex.

6. Overall Determination of Compliance

The Department will base its compliance determination under § 88.41(c) of the regulation upon a determination of the following:

a. Whether the policies of an institution are discriminatory in language or effect; or

b. Whether disparities of a substantial and unjustified nature in the benefits, treatment, services, or opportunities afforded male and female athletes exist in the institution's program as a whole; or

c. Whether disparities in individual segments of the program with respect to benefits, treatment, services, or opportunities are substantial enough in and of themselves to deny equality of athletic opportunity.

11

KENNETH H. BASTIAN JR.

Thank Title IX for Some of That Gold

August 5, 1984

Two significant things happened in 1984 that affected women's sports in America: the Olympics in Los Angeles and the Supreme Court decision in Grove City v. Bell. Despite a boycott led by the Soviet Union (in retaliation for the United States' boycott of the 1980 summer Olympics in Moscow), the Olympic games in Los Angeles brought unprecedented media attention to the contributions American female athletes made to the sporting event. (A similar process would be at work at the 1996 Olympics in Atlanta and the 2004 Olympics in Athens, both of which have often been called "the Title IX Olympics.") Led by outstanding gold-medal performances by gymnast Mary Lou Retton, runner Joan Benoit in the first-ever women's marathon, and basketball star Cheryl Miller, women's medal success seemed a direct reflection of the new opportunities created by Title IX. Miller, for example, developed her basketball skills while on an athletic scholarship at the University of Southern California, and Benoit attended the University of North Carolina on a track scholarship. But the Supreme Court decision in Grove City v. Bell, in which the Court ruled that Title IX applied only to specific programs that received federal funds, not to an entire institution, threatened to derail that progress. In this article, Kenneth H. Bastian Jr., the director of East Coast operations for the Los Angeles Organizing Committee, linked the two events. Joan Benoit put it more pointedly: "It's like dangling a carrot in front of a rabbit, praising the victories then drying up the money."

The whole world is watching American women win Olympic gold medals in Los Angeles, thanks to a dramatic explosion of interest—and money—devoted to women's sports in the United States. As a firm believer in the private sector, and as one who does not advocate government interference where it has no business, I'd be delighted to

---

Kenneth H. Bastian Jr., "Thank Title IX for Some of That Gold," *Washington Post* (August 5, 1984), C7.

report that the catalyst for this growth in women's amateur sports was the same as for me: early encouragement from school athletic programs and generous corporate sponsorships.

Instead, a key reason that Cheryl Miller leads our women's basketball team to one victory after another and that Tracy Caulkins has broken swimming records for our country is that they, like the majority of their teammates, have benefited from a law passed by Congress in 1972.

That law, Title IX of the Education Amendments Act of 1972, states that "no person in the United States shall, on the basis of sex, be excluded from participation in, be denied the benefits of, or be subjected to discrimination under any educational program or activity receiving financial or federal assistance."

It forced American schools, colleges and universities to broaden their women's athletic programs, and led to the first athletic scholarships being made available to women. The results have been dramatic. The number of women in intercollegiate athletic programs jumped from 16,000 in 1972 to over 150,000 today. In 1972 only 7 percent of high school athletes were girls. Ten years later, the number had jumped to 35 percent. The quality, as well as the quantity, of their achievements has been spectacular.

For example, men have taken only seven minutes off their best record marathon running time in the past 10 years. Women, many training seriously for the first time thanks to new women's professional coaches in school programs, have taken an hour and five minutes off their 1964 record. The same story can be told throughout the sports world: women finally are beginning to reach their potential as athletes.

Yet even as we cheer these victories, they may be fleeting. This dramatic increase in female athletic achievement is threatened by the U.S. Supreme Court's ruling in the Grove City College case, which struck down the Title IX provision.

Already schools are relaxing their efforts. According to the Women's Sports Foundation, 23 sex discrimination cases—aimed at forcing compliance with Title IX cases in school athletic programs—have been dropped.

"If an administrator takes it into his head that 'basketball is for boys,' he can do away with girls' basketball with no fear of governmental action," says Donna de Varona, a founding member and president of the Women's Sports Foundation, who won two Olympic gold medals in swimming in 1964.

She knows what the future could hold without Title IX. After her gold medal victories in Tokyo, she had no real opportunities to train in college. However, Don Schollander, her fellow gold medalist, went on to compete for four more years in the highly developed world of men's collegiate swimming.

In the *Grove City* ruling, the Supreme Court found that the equality requirements are "program specific," so that if a college receives $10,000 in federal funds for its mathematics programs, that money must be spent equally for men and women only in mathematics programs. This interpretation allows schools to accept federal dollars through one office while discriminating in another.

Other school programs—including athletics—no longer need to provide equal opportunity if they don't get that direct federal funding. Many schools, therefore, won't have to comply, since their sports are funded from non-federal sources—student fees, alumni groups, ticket sales and television contracts.

Will they voluntarily continue to fund women's sports in a big way? Many believe not, since enough progress hasn't been made yet to elevate women's sports to the same profit-making level as men's sports. Before Title IX, which aimed at promoting the potential of each individual—whether male or female—in sports, athletic directors historically concentrated on whatever program provided the most public attention and revenue for their schools.

College athletic budgets for women, which grew under pressure from Title IX from 1 percent to 16 percent of the total spent on all college sports, probably will shrink again unless Congress acts.

Many of our future Olympic women athletes might have to retire in their teens, like de Varona, while their male counterparts compete for their colleges and universities. Scholarships may dry up. And this may turn out to be the peak year for U.S. women in the Olympics. Of the more than 200 women Olympians representing our nation in the current games, more than 170 received their training in a university or college athletic program.

It is ironic that this progress should be threatened in the same year that finds a woman on the Supreme Court, women aboard the space shuttle, women in the Cabinet and a woman running for vice president. It doesn't have to happen. Both the Democrats and the Republicans, who claim to offer equal opportunity for all Americans, should support legislation that will reinforce the key provisions of Title IX. In a May 22 press conference, the president voiced his support for Title IX, but the language reversing the Grove City College case is currently stalled in the Senate, and time is running out for passage and for our women athletes.

An Increasingly Polarized Debate

12

Cohen et al. v. Brown University
December 22, 1992

Until the 1990s, there was very little case law on Title IX, but that situation began to change with the 1992 Supreme Court decision in Franklin v. Gwinnett County Public Schools *that allowed monetary damages for successful Title IX plaintiffs. Many disputes were settled before going to trial, but Brown University decided to fight when twelve women whose varsity gymnastics and volleyball teams had been dropped to club status, along with the men's golf and water polo teams, sued the university in April 1992. At every stage of the legal battle, which went all the way to the Supreme Court, the plaintiffs prevailed.*

The case began with the plaintiffs requesting a preliminary injunction to reinstate the women's gymnastics and volleyball teams to full varsity status. After hearing fourteen days of testimony, District Court Judge Raymond J. Pettine granted their request. In the decision excerpted here, the judge paid special attention to the three-prong test for determining compliance with Title IX, and found Brown deficient on each count. Pettine's decision was upheld by the U.S. Court of Appeals for the First Circuit in April 1993, setting the stage for a trial on the merits of the case. This trial was also presided over by Judge Pettine, who found in March 1995 that Brown was in violation of Title IX. After another round of appeals in 1996, the Supreme Court declined to hear the case, in effect affirming the lower court decision.

Cohen et al. v. Brown University, 809 F. Supp. 978 (December 22, 1992).

The Three-Part Test

SUBSTANTIAL PROPORTIONALITY

Plaintiffs have demonstrated that Brown does not have a "substantially proportionate" ratio of male and female varsity athletes to their respective undergraduate enrollments. As noted . . . in 1991–92, following the demotion of the four teams, there were 529 men (63.4%) and 305 women (36.6%) in varsity sports. During that year, there were 2917 men (51.8%) and 2716 women (48.2%) enrolled as undergraduates. Thus, Brown fails to satisfy the first question.

PROGRAM EXPANSION

Having failed the requirements of the first question, I must look to the "escape" routes for the university under parts two and three. With respect to the "program expansion" prong, evidence has shown that Brown does not have a continuing practice of program expansion for women athletes, even though it can point to impressive growth in the 1970s. At least since the late 1970s, the undergraduate enrollment at Brown has hovered at roughly 51%–52% men and 48%–49% women. During this period, however, the percentage of participants in the intercollegiate athletic program has remained fairly constant at approximately 61% men and 39% female. Precise numbers were not provided for every year. But according to a 1979 Title IX study internally prepared by Brown, in 1978–79, there were 558 men (63.9%) and 315 women (36.1%) participating on varsity teams. In addition, the only women's team added since 1977 was winter track in 1982, a sport that merely involved providing indoor space to the existing women's track team.

Brown argues that equating "expansion" with increased numerical participation is overly restrictive, and that there is considerable evidence showing growth in the women's athletic program. Among other things, they allege that since the 1970s: (1) coaching for women's teams has consistently improved; (2) more coaches have been added for women's teams; (3) "admissions practices" have helped women gain participation opportunities to a greater degree than men; and (4) the level of competition for women has increased.

Even accepting all of the above statements as true, I still believe that Brown has failed to satisfy the second question in the three-part test. The Policy Interpretation directly links the "program expansion" step to the number of teams and athletes participating in intercollegiate competition, regardless of whether the quality of the program has improved. Thus, I believe, that in assessing compliance with this question, a court must address past actions and future plans to add or eliminate sports, taking into consideration the interests and abilities of the underrepresented sex. This interpretation is consistent with the Investigator's Manual.

INTERESTS AND ABILITIES

Brown has failed questions one and two under the three-part test. I now move on to the last question. With all due respect to defendants' position, I find that in denying full varsity status to the women's volleyball and gymnastics teams, Brown has not accommodated the interests and abilities of women athletes under the existing athletic program. Keeping the two teams at an "intercollegiate club" level is not sufficient to satisfy the third question of the three-part test. If Brown could establish that despite the statistical disparity between the number of men and women participating on varsity teams, there are no other women who want to compete at this level, the university might have a strong defense. Brown might have demonstrated, for example, that it attempted to create new varsity teams, but that there was no interest or ability to play these sports. Or, it might have shown that women have not asked Brown to establish any new varsity teams.

But that is not the case here. Brown is cutting off varsity opportunities where there is great interest and talent, and where Brown still has an imbalance between men and women varsity athletes in relation to their undergraduate enrollments. Both the women's gymnastics and volleyball teams have competed as varsity intercollegiate teams since 1974. More importantly, testimony at the hearing showed that these two teams were viable varsity squads when they were demoted in May 1991. The women's gymnastics team, for example, won the Ivy League championship in 1990. That same year, Eileen Rocchio, one of the plaintiffs, was the individual "all-around" Ivy League gymnastics champion, and was named rookie of the year in the East Coast Athletic Conference. Many of the individual plaintiffs who testified described in detail their dedication to sports and their years of training prior to matriculating at Brown.

Further, some evidence was suggested that other women's teams besides gymnastics and volleyball have been, and continue to be, qualified to compete at the varsity level. At this preliminary stage, I am not in a position to rule definitively on the varsity capabilities of other teams. Nor do I believe that Brown's violation of the three-part test requires it to simply create new women's varsity teams at the request of any students. Rather, Brown may consider the expressed interests of the students, whether there are sufficient numbers of athletes to form a team, and whether there is a reasonable expectation of intercollegiate competition for that team. At the same time, however, as long as men continue to constitute a disproportionate piece of the varsity pie, Brown bears the burden of proof with respect to the second and third components of the three-part test. In my opinion, plaintiffs have shown a sufficient likelihood of success with respect to all three questions. . . .

Conclusion

For all the reasons stated above, Brown University is ordered to take the following actions immediately:

1. Restore women's gymnastics and women's volleyball to their former status as fully funded intercollegiate varsity teams in Brown's intercollegiate athletic program;

2. Provide coaching staff, uniforms, equipment, facilities, publicity, travel opportunities and all other incidentals of an intercollegiate varsity team at Brown to women's gymnastics and women's volleyball on a basis equal to that provided to these teams during the 1990–91 school year;

3. Provide university funding to the two women's teams in an amount equal to that provided to the teams during the 1990–91 school year;

4. Provide an on-campus office, long-distance telephone and clerical support for the head coaches of the two teams, assign admissions liaisons, restore special admissions consideration to the athletic recruits identified by the head coaches, and extend the deadline for filing applications to Brown for such recruits to the same date as the latest accorded to any recruits identified by other intercollegiate varsity teams for 1992–93, or by March 5, 1993, whichever is later; and

5. Prohibit the elimination or reduction in status, or the reduction in the current level of university funding, of any existing women's intercollegiate varsity team until this case is resolved on the merits.

Let me reiterate that I view the restoration of the two women's teams to full varsity status as a temporary solution. If I find at a trial on the merits that Brown has violated Title IX with respect to § 106.41(c)(1), I will leave it to Brown to draw up its own plan for complying with this provision. In short, Brown has the ultimate discretion in how it chooses to structure its intercollegiate athletic program, if it decides to operate one at all, so long as it satisfies the dictates of Title IX.

SO ORDERED:

Raymond J. Pettine
Senior U.S. District Judge

13

AMY COHEN

Winning a Losing Battle
1992

The lead plaintiff in Cohen et al. v. Brown *was a gymnast named Amy Cohen. The decision to cut funding for women's gymnastics and volley-ball and Cohen's subsequent decision to join eleven other women in challenging that decision in court happened during her junior and senior years. Lawsuits generally take a long time to work their way through the courts, so when she graduated from Brown University, the case was just getting underway. She titled this entry in the 1992 Brown yearbook "Winning a Losing Battle," a phrase that foreshadowed how the personal disappointments that she and her teammates faced would in the long run turn into an important victory for women athletes nationwide.*

Fast-forward to Amy Cohen's fifth reunion in 1997. Cohen, now a second grade teacher in Baltimore, returned to Brown a hero, a stark contrast to her senior year, when she often felt shunned by her classmates. Her second graders, who compared her to civil rights pioneer Rosa Parks, immediately grasped the principle behind Title IX even if they didn't know the specifics. "They believe everyone should be treated fairly, and they can't comprehend a world where that doesn't always happen," Cohen said in an interview. "So, yes, they understand Title IX, in a very

Amy Cohen, "Winning a Losing Battle," *Liber Bruniensis* (1992), Brown University Archives, Providence, Rhode Island.

nontechnical way. But, you know, the funny thing is I think they under-
stand it better than most of the nation's athletic directors."

It is hard to put into words what the Brown gymnastics team has meant to me. It has been my heart and soul for the last four years. I will miss gymnastics like I have never missed anything before: the excitement, the tension, the anticipation and frustration, the laughter and silliness, the hard work, and the dedication. I know of no feeling like that of nailing a routine after hours, days, years of practice.

But it is not just the sport that I will miss as I leave Brown, it is the team. The women on the gymnastics team have been much more than just my teammates; they have been my confidants, my advisors, my party buddies, and my study partners. They have helped me through the tough times and shared with me the good times. It is not enough to say that they are my friends. I have found here a group of people with whom I share a bond that I believe no one but another college gymnast could understand.

There have been many highlights for the Brown gymnastics team while I have been here. Winning the Ivy title for the first time ever, getting a new gym, beating Yale, University of Vermont, and Southern Utah, breaking team records on every event, but the accomplishment that I am most proud of is having a team this year. While we lost our funding and our varsity status, we did not lose our spirit and enthusi-asm. During my four years on the gymnastics team, I have learned lessons and gained memories that will last a lifetime.

NATIONAL COLLEGIATE ATHLETIC ASSOCIATION

Final Report of the NCAA Gender-Equity Task Force

July 26, 1993

In 1991, the National Collegiate Athletic Association (NCAA) commissioned its first comprehensive study of the status of female athletes in its member institutions. While not specifically designed to measure compliance with Title IX, the report nonetheless documented undeniable inequities in the resources available to male and female athletes. Translated into dollar figures for schools at the Division I level, the report shows that male athletes received $849,130 in scholarships compared to $372,800 for female athletes; men's programs received $612,206 for operating expenses compared to $179,078 for women's; and on average $139,152 was spent on recruiting male athletes compared to $28,840 for women. In its final report issued in 1993, the NCAA formulated guidelines to achieve gender equity, but still paid lip service to the "male athlete as breadwinner" model of financing athletic programs by encouraging the maintenance of supposedly revenue-producing male sports such as football and basketball.

Definition of Gender Equity

The task force defines gender equity in this manner:

The Association asserts the value of equitable participation and treatment of men and women in intercollegiate athletics through its structure, programs, legislation and policies. It is the responsibility of the Association to act affirmatively to assure equity in the quantity and quality of participation in women's athletics.

At an institutional level, gender equity in intercollegiate athletics describes an environment in which fair and equitable distribution of

---

Final Report of the NCAA Gender-Equity Task Force (Indianapolis: National Collegiate Athletic Association, 1993), 2–5, 9–10.

overall athletics opportunities, benefits and resources is available to women and men and in which student-athletes, coaches and athletics administrators are not subject to gender-based discrimination.

An athletics program can be considered gender equitable when the participants in both the men's and women's sports programs would accept as fair and equitable the overall program of the other gender. No individual should be discriminated against on the basis of gender, institutionally or nationally, in intercollegiate athletics.

Principles of Gender Equity

The following principles are those the Association and its member institutions should follow regarding gender equity. Legislation should be presented to the membership to have these included in the "Principles for Conduct in Intercollegiate Athletics" section of the NCAA Manual.

    a.   It is the responsibility of the Association's members to comply with Federal and state laws regarding gender equity.

    b.   The Association should not adopt legislation that would prevent member institutions from complying with applicable gender-equity laws.

    c.   The Association should adopt legislation to enhance member institutions' compliance with applicable gender-equity laws.

    d.   The activities of the Association should be conducted in a manner free of gender bias.

Guidelines to Promote Gender Equity

The task force has developed the following guidelines to be used to promote and to achieve gender equity.

    a.   Institutions should support intercollegiate athletics participation opportunities for males and females in an equitable manner. The ultimate goal for each institution should be that the numbers of male and female athletes are substantially proportionate to their numbers in the institution's undergraduate student population. Addressing the interests of women athletes, including development of efforts to expand those interests, and continuing efforts to increase opportunities are appropriate pathways for realizing the ultimate goal of substantial proportionality of participation. Thus, the (a) participation, (b) efforts and (c) interests tests of the Title IX regulation are the appropriate tests for equitable participation.

b. An important concern in promoting and achieving gender equity is generating and sustaining the financial resources necessary to support and enhance participation opportunities for women. The history of some institutions is that those resources have been primarily and disproportionately generated by men's sports, usually football and men's basketball. While this fact cannot be used to set those programs outside of gender-equity considerations, it should be understood that, at some institutions, maintaining the revenue-generating capacity of sports, as well as increasing the revenue-generating capacity of women's sports, are essential to enhancing opportunities for women athletes. Maintaining current revenue-producing programs *as one aspect* of long-range planning for increasing women's opportunities is preferable to decreasing the currently provided participation opportunities for men — especially when such maintenance may result in revenues available for both women's and men's programs. Evidence that available resources from revenue-generating activities are equitably distributed to men's and women's programs should be apparent in the evaluation of an institution's planning for gender equity.

c. Proportionally offered opportunities may not yield identically proportionate participation. For example, there may be a difference between men and women in the yield and persistence of participants whether they be recruited scholarship athletes or nonrecruited walk-on athletes. However, institutions should provide equitable encouragement, benefits and opportunities to both groups of student-athletes.

d. Proportionality does not require fixed quotas. Changes over time in interests and abilities and in overall enrollment patterns may yield different patterns of sports sponsorship for both women and men. An institution that is making the appropriate efforts need not be required to make annual changes in the varsity status or support of specific teams simply to achieve numerical precision. Participation interests and abilities of males and females in intercollegiate sport may be different on any individual campus and each sex should be accommodated in light of these differences.

Sports offered for one sex do not have to be identical to sports offered for the other, but participation in *all* sports must be included in determining the appropriate participation levels for men and women.

. . .

Conclusion

While this report, commissioned by our Association, attempts to provide a definition of and steps to the achievement of gender equity in intercollegiate athletics, it is the responsibility of individual colleges and universities to pursue that goal earnestly. In the task force's deliberations, two questions persisted: how can increased opportunities for women be funded, and how can provision of increased opportunities be assured?

The responsibility for providing necessary financial resources falls to individual institutions, just as does funding for all aspects of higher education. And, as in other programs, that responsibility must reside with the institutions' governing bodies, not just athletics departments. The facts that these are difficult economic times or that difficult decisions must be made are true, but they do not alter that responsibility. Chief executive officers and governing boards, and legislatures must identify the resources necessary to provide equal opportunity to all students.

Assurance of equitable treatment and opportunity for women must come from each institution. Enforcement of fairness may not be easy, but it is clearly necessary. The task force heard testimony about what is likely to happen if institutions cannot find a way to assure equity: the courts are currently enforcing adherence to the law, and Congress, as well as the Office for Civil Rights, appear prepared to monitor compliance as well.

We hope and believe that continued court judgments, new legislation and heightened governmental oversight will not be necessary. From the outset, subscribing to fundamentally fair principles in its programs was correctly described as a moral obligation for NCAA members. If, having recognized and documented that our members have neither achieved the spirit of gender equity nor complied with the letter of the law, we fail to act to ameliorate those conditions, others will be justified in finding means to do so. We call upon the membership to do what is right for all student-athletes.

15

CYNTHIA LEE A. PEMBERTON

One Woman's Fight for Gender Equity in Sport

2002

When Cynthia Pemberton was hired at Linfield College in Oregon in 1989 as an assistant athletic director for women's sports, she did not plan to be a Title IX crusader. In fact, she later admitted sheepishly, she had never heard of the law. When she did learn of it in 1992, she first tried to work within her department to raise questions of gender equity and Title IX compliance. In 1995, Pemberton's complaints were still unanswered, and after being "reassigned" away from her job as assistant athletic director, she filed suit against Linfield. Two years later, after intense personal recriminations and substantial financial costs, the case was settled out of court.

In More Than a Game: One Woman's Fight for Gender Equity in Sport *(2002), Pemberton tells the story of her crusade to make Linfield College live up to Title IX's commitment to gender equity in sports. These excerpts describe her arrival on campus, her growing awareness of a problem not being addressed, and her frustrations with male administrators when she brought it to their attention. The selection concludes with her retrospective thoughts about whether it was worth it and whether she would do it again.*

Professionally, I don't think I could have been happier. I've always been a hard worker and an overachiever. Those first years at Linfield were wonderful and fed my insatiable need to be challenged. I was enamored with my job, especially coaching, and readily put in the work needed to excel.

I loved working with college athletes and enjoyed coaching both women and men. I worked like a crazy person. I'd leave for work at 4:30 in the morning and come home between 10:00 and 11:00 at night.

Cynthia Lee A. Pemberton, *More Than a Game: One Woman's Fight for Gender Equity in Sport* (Boston: Northeastern University Press, 2002), 8–9, 18–20, 21–22, 23–24, 25, 27–28, 279–81.

Most of the time I worked six to seven days a week, and I thrived on it. In just a few short years, the Linfield swim program grew from a fledgling start of two women and four men, with no national qualifiers, to one of the premier small-college programs in the country. It was an exciting time.

In my role as assistant athletic director, I was left to my own devices. For the most part, the athletic director (Ad Rutschman) was preoccupied with coaching football, and what time and attention he had to spare were directed toward administering the men's sport programs. Even though I was technically his assistant, we operated independently. We'd meet periodically; I went to him with questions from time to time, but for the most part he left me to do the job of administering and directing women's athletics, which was fine with me.

I don't work well when I feel I'm being controlled. I am a self-starter and an independent worker. I'm good at solving problems and figuring out how to get something done, whom to contact, what resources are needed, and how to get them. I like being given general guidelines about what is to be accomplished and then turned loose to do it. For a while that was Ad's and my mode of operation and, as a result, early on we were quite compatible. It wasn't until a few years later that I realized our relationship was dependent upon my willingness to agree with him, and didn't have much to do with compatibility.

An early example of my willingness to agree with Ad involved a discussion about athletic shoes. The question was whether I had a problem with the men's basketball team being given team shoes while the women's team had to buy their own. I don't remember whether the shoes were being donated, or whether the department was going to purchase them. What I do remember was my response. I said, "If and when the women's basketball team starts making money, they too can have shoes, but until then as long as the men's programs are making the money, it's okay with me that they get more." It's embarrassing. No, it's more than embarrassing; it's appalling that I thought, said, and believed those words. That was me then.

I'd spent my athletic life benefiting from Title IX, and I hadn't had a clue it existed, let alone what it was about. I wasn't a women's sports advocate; I was one of women's sports' worst nightmares, and I didn't even know it. . . .

During the summer of 1992, I received a copy of the regional newsletter *The Inside Track*, a publication of the Oregon Women's Sports Leadership Network. The newsletter was addressed to the athletic director but was forwarded to me, probably from Ad. That newsletter, along with news clips from the *Oregonian* headlining the twenty-year anniversary of Title IX, marked my first real awareness of gender-equity issues, an awareness that would irrevocably change my life and set off a firestorm at Linfield College. On July 27, 1992, I sent the following memo to Ad:

> Ad, the issue of Title IX and Gender Equity in Athletics is making a strong resurgence as we round the 20 year bend of Title IX implementation. The attached articles talk in some detail about Equity Issues.
>
> It is my belief, that although the financial and opportunity status of women's athletics at Linfield has made considerable strides over the past few years, that we still have a ways to go. I think it will be important for us to work together and stay on top of the issues of Gender Equity and Title IX compliance. It is my hope we will take a positive leadership role in pursuing Gender Equity, rather than waiting for compliance pressures to force us to make uncomfortable changes.
>
> I have ordered a copy of the "Title IX Tool Box," a publication that addresses the "meat" of the law, and compliance. Once I receive it, I will review it carefully and then hope we can meet to discuss where we are and where we need to go with women's athletics at Linfield.

I also sent copies of this memo and the attached materials to Charles Walker and Vivian Bull (the outgoing and incoming college presidents), as well as to various Linfield deans and vice presidents. I proceeded as I said I would. I ordered a copy of the *Title IX Tool Box* and began researching and reading about Title IX.

The more I learned, the more I became convinced that the intercollegiate athletics status quo at Linfield was not okay. I didn't realize that I'd opened Pandora's box, and there would be no going back. I thought that Linfield's gender-equity problems were a result of ignorance and naïveté. I figured that if I hadn't known about Title IX, its compliance requirements and potential impact, then others probably hadn't known either. I thought that once we all became educated on the matter, everyone would see the obvious inequities and promptly do the right thing.

There is a warning in the *Title IX Tool Box* that reads something like this: before you start inquiring about and/or pushing for Title IX compliance and gender equity, try to imagine the worst possible response scenario. Try to imagine how bad it could possibly be, and then know it will be worse. I probably would not have chosen to act differently, but I would have been more prepared had I heeded that warning. . . .

As I learned more about Title IX, I began to question Linfield's athletic policies and practices, which just wasn't done under Ad's leadership. To Ad a query was a threat. I found Ad an interesting character: not a bad guy really, just a relic who couldn't seem to change with time. He was a silver-haired ex-athlete, a die-hard football coach with a warm smile and a hot temper who seemed to have grown so accustomed to absolute obedience that anything less was simply intolerable.

An early example of my questioning Ad's status quo occurred in September 1992, and involved a discussion about concession stand use. Our policy and practice then was that a particular men's sport booster (a financial supporter of the athletic program) was in charge of running the concession stand. According to Ad, this booster had funded and built the concession building, and, thus, concessions could be run only when the booster wanted to run them. If the booster didn't want to run concessions during women's events, he didn't have to. The women would simply go without.

On October 5, 1992, I sent Ad, along with various Linfield administrators, my first Title IX overview and program report. . . .

The report itself contained sections on what Title IX actually said; a brief historical overview of its legislation and evolution; copies of the Federal Register Rules and Regulations and Policy Interpretations, which detail how Title IX is to be instituted; and information about Title IX compliance assessment. The report also briefly identified areas of possible compliance concerns that were specific to Linfield athletics.

I'd identified areas of concern in almost every compliance assessment category. First, we weren't allocating athletic financial assistance in proportion to athletic participation. Second, I believed we had problems in regard to the interest and abilities three-prong test; that is, (1) our athletic participation ratios were not proportional to our enrollment ratios; (2) although various women's and men's sports had been added and deleted, we could not show a history and continuing practice of program expansion for women; and (3) we were not fully and effectively accommodating the expressed interest and abilities of existing female athletes: we had club sports and intramurals that indicated both interest and ability in varsity women's sports we did not offer. Third, I identified areas of inequity in almost all of the eleven program components (equipment and supplies, scheduling of games and practice, travel and per diem allowance, tutoring, coaches, locker rooms, practice and competition facilities, medical and training facilities, housing and dining facilities, publicity, recruitment of student-athletes, and support services).

I concluded the report by suggesting that we carefully review our current athletic programs, enact immediate changes where identified inequities could be remedied with minimal cost, and develop a plan to address costlier, long-range change.

My summary statement read:

> While it appears that we do have areas where immediate attention needs to be directed, as well as a need for careful long range planning regarding overall Title IX legal compliance, I am certain we would all agree that Linfield provides the type of environment in which we can take positive steps to assure compliance with the law. By initiating our own evaluative and planful compliance steps, we can avoid the time, cost and negative publicity that an outside evaluation and complaint would entail. Given the current climate of Title IX interest and awareness the likelihood of eventual outside evaluation and intervention could be a definitive possibility. I am sure we are all in agreement that it is in the best interest of Linfield College to be in compliance with the law. . . .

On October 29, more than three weeks after receiving the report, Ad commented, and he was furious! He didn't like copies of the report being sent to others and felt I hadn't followed the chain of command by distributing it as I had. Ad went on to tell me that any Title IX violations at Linfield were my fault, and that it was my job to submit women's sports needs to reflect a move toward equity. In reality Ad was right about my job. Both our job descriptions stated that we were responsible for making sure Linfield athletics complied with federal laws and NAIA rules. Without even knowing it, by reviewing our Title IX compliance and submitting the report, I was doing my job. . . .

Even now, years after writing the original report, as I reread it I am amazed at the degree to which Ad and Scott [Carnahan, Linfield's facility director and head baseball coach] were upset. The report was factual; it wasn't inflammatory. I probably should have expected the response I got, but I didn't. I just couldn't understand why they were so upset. Scott stopped talking to me almost altogether. In fact, he wouldn't even acknowledge my presence with a superficial hello. Both he and Ad were openly hostile, suspicious, and accusatory in their interactions with me and about me.

I didn't really understand then what I understand now. The change implied by that first report and all the various reports, consultations, and meetings that followed meant that much of what they believed in, the very foundation of athletics as they understood it and had lived it, was called into question. For Ad in particular—a moral pillar of the community and small college football coaching legend—if I was right about Title IX and Linfield's lack of compliance, then he and much of what he'd done for the past quarter century was wrong. Not to mention that for Ad, it was always a zero-sum game. He couldn't see it any other way. If women were to get more, then men would get less. Less would mean less winning, less glory, less excellence, less, less, less—and that just wasn't an option. . . .

There are three things I am often asked. The first is how I was able to recall events in such detail. The answer is that I wrote everything down. . . .

The second and third questions are was it worth it and would I do it all again. Those are much tougher questions.

The real cost of equity, the price of Title IX, goes far beyond dollars and cents. I lost a significant part of my job, and, although it took me a while to come to terms with it, my life at Linfield was over. I lost any hope of a career in athletic administration, particularly in the Pacific Northwest, something at the time I thought I wanted. My academic work was hindered and disrupted, and my dissertation focus, after months of work, had to be redirected. I was publicly humiliated over and over again. My swimmers and assistant coaches were harassed and hurt. My reputation in coaching was tainted, my swim camps suffered, and my colleagues in coaching were badgered and scrutinized because of their association with me. Friends and colleagues at Linfield brave enough to stand beside me were also harassed and hurt. Tim [author's husband] was hassled professionally and personally, and I know, although he never complained, my constant neediness wore him down. My Title IX battle cost us both more than one long-standing friendship. I came to the brink of financial ruin. My physical, mental, and emotional health to this day are under repair. The emotionally strong, capable, and resilient woman I once was is less strong, less resilient, and much more vulnerable.

Contrary to popular myth, I haven't retired to a life of leisure in some tropical paradise. But benefits also reach beyond dollars and cents. I believe that women in sport at Linfield benefited from my efforts, and that they continue to benefit, although according to Linfield's annual EADA reports, progress seems to have slowed considerably since my departure. At least locally, awareness regarding gender equity was heightened, and surely there is value in standing up for what is right, not only because it's right, but because it's important to model that behavior for others. And perhaps through this account women and girls in sport will benefit more broadly. . . .

Great strides have been made in gender equity, and it is because of Title IX. But there remains much work to be done. We have not yet achieved equity, and we cannot afford to pull back.

So I suppose the answer is yes, it was worth it, and I would do it all again. But if I have regrets, they are that I remained so naively optimistic for so long and, as a result, was surprised, confused, and hurt, over and over again. Even now there is a part of me that doesn't understand, that just doesn't get it.

It should be a simple concept. Inattention and resistance to gender equity is morally, ethically, and legally wrong. The only way to make sense of Linfield's legacy of wrongdoing is to assume that, like me (before the summer of 1992), people at Linfield hadn't known any better, and that once they knew better, we would work together to make things right. The alternative is to assume that Linfield, and the hundreds of schools across the country that continue to ignore and openly resist gender equity do know better, and that their actions and inactions were and are intentional and willful.

16

U.S. HOUSE OF REPRESENTATIVES

*Hearing before the Subcommittee
on Postsecondary Education, Training,
and Life-long Learning of the Committee on
Economic and Educational Opportunities*

May 9, 1995

In 1995, Congress scheduled yet another round of hearings about the scope and implementation of the law. Although lawmakers talked about presenting varying perspectives and seeking a balanced discussion, it is clear that the battle lines were being more starkly drawn. On one side were advocates

Hearing on Title IX of the Education Amendments Act of 1972: Hearing before the Subcommittee on Postsecondary Education, Training, and Life-long Learning of the Committee on Economic and Educational Opportunities, House of Representatives, 104th Cong., 1st sess., May 9, 1995.

of women's athletics, who applauded the progress that women had made, but complained that gender equity was still a far distant goal. On the other side were those who claimed that Title IX had gone too far. More specifically, critics charged that men, especially in the so-called men's minor sports, were losing as women gained. With college athletics viewed as a zero-sum proposition, attempts to find a middle ground were increasingly lost in rhetoric that literally pitted sons against daughters.

The following excerpts demonstrate the divide. Taken together, they show the range of opinions about the successes and problems associated with Title IX after the law had been in effect for more than two decades. They also show strong continuities with many of the opinions expressed in the 1975 hearings (Document 5).

Statement of J. Dennis Hastert, Representative from Illinois

Thank you, Mr. Chairman. I certainly very much appreciate the opportunity to speak this morning and to thank you for your interest and help in holding this hearing.

I was interested in hearing the opening statements this morning. I understand that there are political threats out there and sometimes, when people make political threats, it is probably not wise to tread on that ground. But you know I have watched Title IX.

I started coaching in high school in 1965 when women didn't have an opportunity to go out for organized athletics. All there was at that time was a GAA, a Girls Athletic Association, and they didn't really have traveling teams and the ability to do that. So I appreciate what Title IX has done for women and girls in this country. I think it has been a wonderful opportunity for women to be able to participate and become involved in athletics and to have the same experience that men have had previous to 1972.

But sometimes when we put laws forward and bring laws forward, especially from the basic intent of what that law was to how it develops, there are "unintended consequences." I think that is one of the things that should be examined. For instance, in my good friend Mr. Williams' district, which is all of Montana, great wrestling programs are being threatened, and we need to take a look at that. I don't think that was ever the intent of Title IX.

You know, my interest in this issue surrounding Title IX of the Education Amendments of 1972 has been fostered in many ways. First, I am a former coach. I coached both wrestling and football for 16 years at a small high school. I married a women's athletic coach who is still teaching elementary P.E. after 29 years. I love seeing young men and young women involved in athletics because I know what they get out of it. I think a lot of the kids I coached during those 16 years and the opportunities that they have had. I was the President of the only wrestling coaches association in 1975 and 1976, and I traveled to Washington several times when the Amateur Sports Act was moving through the Congress to make sure that grassroots had a say in organized athletics in this country.

Secondly, in the last year I have received hundreds of letters from youngsters around this Nation who are no longer able to participate in sports because their sport is being eliminated at the various universities that they attend. I have heard from kids from San Francisco University in California—kids from California all the way to Pennsylvania. They don't understand how schools can promise them an opportunity to compete and later drop those programs in the middle of their eligibility. They don't understand the policy fixes of what is going on. . . .

The oldest sport known to man is disappearing faster than any other. Some people say it is due to a "lack of interest," but that is not true because wrestling is growing in the elementary and secondary levels faster than any other comparative sport.

It was not hard to notice that this trend was getting out of hand in my own State. Western Illinois University dropped its wrestling programs a couple of years ago, ostensibly to make room for women's athletics. The University of Illinois dropped its men's swim team program, resulting in a lawsuit alleging reverse discrimination. Northern Illinois University, in my own Congressional district, proposed to eliminate wrestling and swimming last fall at the urging of the OCR. Eastern Illinois University followed closely behind with an announcement to drop wrestling and swimming.

President David Jorns from Eastern is here today to tell you about their experiences. Most recently, Illinois State University has announced its intention to eliminate wrestling and soccer. This is just in the State of Illinois in the last year or so, but it is happening all across the United States.

When sports are eliminated, the universities cite their need to comply with Title IX and the proportionality rules as part or all of their reason. While I want all schools to comply with Title IX, I strongly believe that the elimination of opportunities for anyone was not the intent of Title IX. These lost opportunities are what I call the "unintended consequences" of Title IX. . . .

The benefits of sports in general—the values of fair play and team-work, of stretching yourself to the fullest and pushing your mind and body to its utmost performance—will be lost on these women and men who will not get the opportunity they should have. They are caught in the "unintended consequences" of Title IX. They are caught in a quota system which makes them a number, not an athlete. It is not what Congress intended, and it should not be allowed to continue. . . .

However, maybe we need to think in broader terms, to find a way to encourage Title IX compliance without the use of quotas. We do not assume that everyone who enrolls in a university wants the opportunity to be in the band. Let's face it, not everyone wants to play the tuba or the piano. But we operate under similar assumptions when we consider athletics. Proportionality, at the very least, should be based on those in the interested population rather than everyone enrolled. I urge the committee to consider creative solutions to ending the continuing discrimination out there without using proportionality.

Finally, I challenge all of us to think about whether Congress intended for Title IX to result in the elimination of athletic opportunities for anyone. Can any of us say that we want Title IX to be implemented in such a way?

It really disturbs me to hear people claim that it is fine to cut opportunities for men to eradicate discrimination. Well, Mr. Chairman, that is *not* fine. That view represents everything that is wrong about Title IX. When a law ceases to work for positive improvements and simply becomes a way to get back at the system that perpetrated discrimination, we have lost our focus on what it means to work toward gender equity. It doesn't help anyone just to keep tearing the future of these kids out from under them.

I hope this hearing will lay the groundwork for some positive changes to our present system of Title IX. And thank you very much for your attention.

Statement of Christine H. B. Grant, Representative for the National Association of Collegiate Women Athletics Administrators

Thank you for providing me with the opportunity to comment on the status of intercollegiate athletic programs across the nation and the need for continued strong support of the current Title IX legislation and interpretation. . . .

From the late 1800's until 1972, men at the intercollegiate level enjoyed all of the varsity participation slots in the nation, opportunities often financially supported by both institutional funds as well as student fees from both male and female students. Thus, at many institutions, women were not only denied the opportunity to participate in varsity sports, they were also required to financially support the athletic opportunities for men! Any woman who desired to participate in club sports (the highest level of sport available to women) then had to pay for these opportunities out of their pockets again. Of course, men in varsity sports had all expenditures paid for them and, in addition, most received a totally free education, which today costs anywhere up to $100,000 each.

Although Title IX passed 23 years ago, men still command the lion's share of all sporting opportunities. The 1992 NCAA Gender Equity Study shows that women received only 29% of the participation opportunities and 28% of all athletic scholarships. In most instances student fees from women undergraduates are still used to support more than twice as many participation slots for men as women. Would such biased practices be accepted in any other area of our universities? I think not. What an injustice! What a farce it makes of both the letter and the spirit of federal law!

Rather than having hearings to determine how to protect football, our Congress should be having hearings on what must be done immediately to end these discriminatory practices at all levels of our educational institutions, that are, supposedly, equally committed to both young women and young men. We are not talking about professional sport here; we are talking about giving youngsters an equal opportunity to experience the joys, the challenges and the educational lessons of sport that directly contribute to their growth and development as people.

I primarily fault the Chief Executive Officers at our educational institutions for the current situation. For more than two decades, they have known the requirements of the Federal law and could have moved gradually into compliance. Far too many chose to take as long as they could to do as little as possible. In recent years, there has been a resurgence of a demand by female student-athletes for equal opportunities, coinciding with a time in which most universities found themselves in financial difficulties. Many hoped that the CEOs, through the NCAA Presidents Commission, would mandate cost-containment measures in intercollegiate athletics, especially in Division I. They could have eliminated the excesses in football and men's basketball and demanded reform of our costly recruiting system. On a national level, we could, for example, prohibit these teams from staying in hotels the night before home games; we could also drastically reduce their flashy 200-page media guides. These are but two examples of practices which cause 73% of the entire men's budget to go to these two sports. Through a proactive stance, the CEOs could have averted the current situation which now pits men's minor sports against women's sports (the have-nots against the have-nots), leaving intact enormous football and basketball expenditures and deficits. Blaming gender equity for the demise of men's minor sports is a red herring; they are being dropped because CEOs will not address the problem of habitual excessive spending, either on the institutional or the national level.

Although few schools have achieved compliance with Federal law, it can be done. I am happy to share with you an impressive list of institutions that have made the commitment to equal opportunity and are progressing toward that goal without dropping men's sports. The list reveals that lack of opportunity, not lack of interest has kept women from participating in intercollegiate athletics. If, at a national level, we can cooperate to achieve real cost containment in the areas I have mentioned, I am convinced that we will be able to accomplish three important goals:

a. expanding women's participation opportunities
b. retaining men's minor sports
c. balancing athletic budgets

Given the facts I have presented today coupled with the additional data in my written testimony, it is preposterous for us to be considering anything other than expanding the opportunities for women to participate in sport. Equitable sporting opportunities for women can and must be realized, or none of us will be able to look our daughters or granddaughters in the eye to explain "why not."

Statement of T. J. Kerr, President
of the National Wrestling Coaches Association

INTRODUCTION

Mr. Chairman and members of the Subcommittee, I am T. J. Kerr, wrestling coach at California State University at Bakersfield and President of the National Wrestling Coaches Association (NWCA). I am honored and privileged that you selected me to address you today about a crisis within our athletic community.

The NWCA is the voice of all wrestling coaches in the country. I shall also attempt to speak on behalf of all the young male athletes in this nation and their parents. We are particularly concerned about the tens of thousands of young men whose athletic careers have already been cut short by the OCR rules.

While we firmly agree with the letter and spirit of Title IX, we are firmly committed to the proposition that it is unconscionable to eliminate male programs or male athletes to satisfy a gender quota. Both the OCR and the courts have expressed the opinion that a school is justified in dropping male athletes in order to comply with Title IX. We believe that this opinion misconstrues Congressional intent.

We are today therefore petitioning Congress seeking relief from the draconian but unintended consequences of Title IX as interpreted and enforced by the OCR and the courts.

IS THERE A CRISIS?

As a threshold issue, you might ask—is there a crisis? Yes there is. Male gymnastics is almost extinct at the college level. Wrestling has relatively recently lost over 100 programs and may lose as many as 20 programs this year.

Programs in every sport have been dropped or reduced in number—soccer, baseball, tennis, swimming, etc.—even football and basketball.

WHY IS THERE A CRISIS?

All male sports programs are at risk because of the proportionality rule/gender quota which the OCR has drafted. There are about 190,000 male college athletes in Divisions I, II, and III. There are about 105,000 female athletes. How can proportionality be achieved when the present male to female ratio is 47–53? If the trend continues, administrators will have to eliminate about 100,000 male athletes to reach proportionality.

In 1972 when Congress enacted Title IX the college enrollment ratio nationally was 55%+ male. By the 21st Century 55% of the college population may well be female. The 55–45 female-to-male ratio sets up a gender quota which is impossible to achieve in no small part because females do not tend to compete in sports—particularly those like football and wrestling. Nor do they participate in a non-scholarship/walk-on capacity in any where near the number which males do. California Bakersfield, for example, we are 62% female by enrollment. Statistically, it is almost impossible with that enrollment ratio to have a viably diverse athletics program for male students.

HOW DOES PROPORTIONALITY CAUSE ELIMINATION?

Elimination of male athletes occurs in two ways—administrators eliminate programs and/or they eliminate *non-scholarship/walk-on athletes* from those programs. Both are anathema. We have one goal—We seek to end the elimination or reduction of male sports programs to achieve a quota.

School administrators believe that they must achieve proportionality. Many are unable, because of budget constraints, to add female sports programs, so these administrators drop male programs or "cap" sports by dropping the non-scholarship or walk-on athlete.

Both of these approaches to achieving "gender equity" are wrong. Programs should not be eliminated because athletes matriculate at a school in the good faith belief that the administration will honor its commitment to provide a program for their four years of college. It is a devastating betrayal for these young men when they learn that their faith has been misplaced. It is worse when they are informed that the reason for the elimination of their program is Title IX or gender equity.

The capping of male sports is equally discriminatory and destructive. In this circumstance a young man pays tuition, walks on to a team, works as hard as the first-teamer, but simply does not have the skills to compete at the highest levels. These athletes normally are the best students and the best contributors to their alma maters when they graduate. More importantly, they are comparatively free to the school. The school dumps them because they are the most expendable. . . .

WHAT IS THE IMPACT OF THE GENDER QUOTA ON OUR NEXT GENERATION OF MALE ATHLETES?

I have sought in my program to work with the many young men who otherwise would not be able to attend college, and I know I speak for the coaches of all male programs when I say that the elimination of male opportunities will greatly affect the future generation of young men.

All statistics reflect that the opportunities existing for females is much greater than for males. For example, wrestling is the sixth most popular high school sport in the nation. There is, however, only one college program for every 33 high school wrestling programs (33–1).

Of the top ten female sports, the worst ratio is about 22–1 and the best ratio is about 11–1. High school females have greater opportunities to compete at the collegiate level in every counterpart sport except golf and gymnastics.

As these disparities continue to grow as male programs are eliminated, high school and junior high school male programs will atrophy and die. Many kids, without the option of participating in athletics, will choose antisocial activities.

Unfortunately, at present, there is hardly a male high school athlete who is unaware of Title IX and the OCR's approach to gender equity. Expectedly, these males are angry and their morale is sinking. . . .

WHAT CAN BE DONE TO SOLVE THE PROBLEM?

First, things have changed since 1972 when Title IX was enacted. Female athletic participation has skyrocketed from about 10% to about 40% of the total collegiate athletic community. These enormous changes occurred in the face of the fact that football, a non-counterpart sport, absorbs over 1/4 of all of the male participation slots.

"Gender equity" is a reality in almost every school in the country. As proof, one need only reflect on the fact that females now have nearly the same number of college athletic programs as males (6520–7211 respectively) and receive more scholarship aid in almost every counterpart sport.

Gender equity, however, should not be synonymous with gender quotas. The OCR's gender quota, which masquerades as the proportionality rule, is now an anachronism which should be abolished.

In its place, reason should prevail. Schools offering the same number of athletic programs to males and females should be deemed to be in compliance with Title IX. Since there are nearly the same number of athletic programs presently for males and females, schools should be encouraged to build up the present programs rather than creating new ones.

Also, in that males participate in a non-scholarship/walk-on capacity in much greater numbers than females, it is time to require females to fill these "unused participatory opportunities" which if developed, would solve this problem alone.

CONCLUSION

In conclusion, Mr. Chairman, thank you for holding this hearing to consider our petition. I know that when you created Title IX you did not intend the elimination of male sports as we know them—that, however, will be the unintended consequence if Congress does not intervene. We need your help to change the rules so that we can exist and make gender equity work for both males and females.

Finally, thank you for the opportunity to appear here today. I will be happy to answer to the best of my ability any questions you may have of me.

Statement of Wendy Hilliard, President of the Women's Sports Foundation

I am Wendy Hilliard, currently the President of the Women's Sports Foundation, a 501(c)(3) non-profit educational organization. The Foundation was founded in 1974 by Billie Jean King, Donna de Varona, Wyomia Tyus and other champion female athletes to promote and enhance sports and fitness opportunities for girls and women. These successful women athletes did not want girls following in their footsteps to face the same barriers to participation as they did. To address the needs of girls and women in sports, the Foundation produces programming in four areas: education, advocacy, recognition and opportunity.

I am also an athlete. My sport is rhythmic gymnastics. An Olympic event since 1984, it combines hand apparatus such as a hoop, ball, or a flowing ribbon with gymnastics floor moves and music. I was the first African-American to represent this sport in international competition, which I did for almost ten years including three World Championships. I won international gold medals and was twice National Team Captain.

I went to college in the 1980s when Title IX was supposedly in force. My sport wasn't offered at the varsity level. I did not receive an athletic scholarship. I had to work my way through college, and pay for my athletic training, yet graduated from New York University with honors. The month before graduation, I missed the 1988 Olympic trials by .05 of a point. Why didn't I, as one of the best in the entire country in my sport, and at the top of my class as a student have the opportunity for an athletic scholarship? There are still many women who are asking that question today. Twenty-three years after the passage of Title IX, women are still receiving only 35% of all college athletic participation opportunities.

On many occasions I wonder, what if? But, the fact is, my lack of opportunity has given me more resolve to support equal opportunities for females in sport, which is why I am speaking before you today. . . .

COMMON QUESTIONS RAISED ABOUT TITLE IX
AS IT AFFECTS COLLEGE ATHLETIC PROGRAMS

The Women's Sports Foundation's primary mission is education. We believe it is important for the general public and Congress to know the facts rather than be guided by popular mythology and misconceptions promoted by those who oppose Title IX. Thus, I would like to address issues often raised in discussion about the law.

Do men's non-revenue sports have to be eliminated in order for schools to comply with Title IX?

The purpose of laws prohibiting discrimination is to bring the disadvantaged population up to the level of the advantaged population, not to treat men's minor sports like women's sports who weren't given a chance to play. If we are going to expand opportunities for women to participate in athletics without cutting men's non-revenue sports such as wrestling, swimming and gymnastics, there has to be a reduction of current expenditures on existing men's teams and a transfer of those resources to women's programs.

 If we all agree that participation opportunities and direct educational benefits to student-athletes are the most important reasons for maintaining athletic programs in higher education, then other cost-saving and revenue-producing measures will be pursued prior to cutting teams or reducing squad sizes. It is unconscionable that colleges and universities are not considering or implementing some or all of the following revenue-producing or cost-cutting measures before cutting men's teams:

1. Increase revenues of men's minor sports and women's sports at the institutional and conference level. The women's sports market is virtually untapped and must be developed. According to Fulks's study of *Revenues and Expenses in Intercollegiate Athletics* (NCAA, 1994), there are at least 16 Division IA institutions in 1993 that had women's programs which generated $900,000 dollars or more. There is also evidence to indicate that the spectator and donor market for women's sports is a new market—different from that supporting men's athletics. Therefore, developing that new market will not put women's sports in a competitive position against an institution's own men's program.

2. Add a 12th football game or extra basketball game and designate all revenues for gender equity.

3. Encourage conference members to adopt the same sports when expanding women's programs in order to realize the financial savings of competition within a reasonable geographic proximity.
4. Create leaner administrative structures at the institutional and conference levels (institutions pay for conference operating expenses).
5. Delay the construction and renovation of athletics facilities. It is absurd for an institution out of compliance with Title IX to be spending $120,000 to change the wood in the head football coach's office from oak to mahogany.
6. Eliminate the use of cellular phones.
7. Severely limit off-campus recruiting activities. We can no longer afford to spend $15,000–25,000 to recruit one basketball player.
8. Eliminate housing athletics teams in hotels prior to *home* contests.
9. Eliminate spring break trips to southern states.
10. Have every team eliminate their farthest away game and replace it with a contest within a 90 mile radius of campus.
11. Have every team cut their schedule by one contest.
12. Reduce the use of charter airplanes and airplane travel over short distances.
13. Prohibit glossy, 4-color cover media guides and recruiting materials.
14. Have the institution change its competitive division to one requiring lower expenditures (i.e., Division IA moving to IAA, IAA moving to II, II moving to III (non-scholarship). It is not right that the "status" of a higher competitive division is more important than the opportunity to play.

And there are many more examples like the above of what can be done to cut costs. The NCAA and conferences of like institutions should legislate many of these reductions in order to ensure a level playing field.

Many institutions will choose to cut a men's sport rather than reduce the "standard of living" of men's football or basketball and will blame the need on gender equity rather than excessive and unnecessary men's sport expenditures. Congress and the public must question such actions. Cutting participation

opportunities for men should be the last choice as a method of achieving gender equity.

Are women less interested in playing sports than men?

There are those who would persuade the committee to conclude that women aren't as interested in athletic opportunities as men citing lower participation numbers in NCAA member institutions, the lack of "walk-ons" on women's teams and lower participation numbers in high school sports.

The issue of interest of female athletes is a critical one. **Opportunity drives interest and ability.** Title IX's purpose includes redressing historic discrimination. **There is no lack of interest and ability on the part of males or females to participate in the finite number of opportunities available at the collegiate level.**

It is important to understand that colleges and universities can only afford to support a fraction of the sport opportunities it would take to meet the interest and ability of either men or women. Currently, there are approximately 189,642 male and 105,532 female athletes on NCAA teams (NCAA, 1994). Those limited participation slots are being competed for by over 3.4 million males and 2 million female athletes participating at the high school level (in a system that itself does not yet provide full equal opportunity for girls) and there are many more girls participating in Olympic sports traditionally not offered in the high school athletic program. There will never be a lack of interest or ability on the part of males or females. The real question is how do you demonstrate that the schools' limited opportunities to participate are apportioned in a fair manner. . . .

There are those who say that if the size of men's sports teams are capped, minority athlete walk-ons in football and track will be most adversely affected. New women's sports will cater to a predominantly white population. Is this true?

There are those who would stoop to allege that supporting gender equity is supporting racism. Gender equity and sport segregation are two very important but separate issues.

It doesn't make sense to argue that keeping football teams large is the way to address the issue of sport segregation. Such a contention would support the continuation of football, basketball and track as minority ghettos and not address the real problem of discrimination and lack of encouragement of minorities in other sports.

Race and gender discrimination are equally important issues that demand the focused attention of educators. It is ridiculous to suggest that gender equity efforts should stop until sport integration occurs. Such a position results in pitting two victims of discrimination against each other: women and racial minorities.

SUMMARY

Your interest and actions in maintaining Title IX as it is currently written is very important. When women are only halfway toward equal opportunity in sport twenty-three years after the law was adopted, it is obvious that now is not the time to take a step backward. It is the time to encourage more federal efforts to enforce the law. We cannot as a nation tolerate discriminatory treatment on the basis of gender. We must prepare our daughters as well as we prepare our sons. We must give them the same educational benefits. If sport belongs in higher education, intercollegiate athletics, including football, must conform to the requirements of Title IX of the 1972 Education Amendments Act.

College football coaches and institutions who do not wish to comply with Title IX are asking the public to choose between gender equity and football. We should never be asked to choose between our sons and our daughters.

A simple analogy may be helpful. You are a parent who has a son and a daughter. For many years, you have given your son, on the occasions of his birthday and holidays, baseballs, gloves, footballs, hockey sticks and other sports equipment. His room is full of sports implements—a veritable palace of athletics privilege. One day, your daughter comes to you complaining that her brother won't let her borrow his glove so she can have a catch with her girlfriends. Would you tell her to go out and work so she can buy her own glove or would you explain to your son how important it is to share? Would you change your commitment to the importance of sharing and treating your children equally if your son advanced the argument that his sister would destroy, lose or in some other way damage his glove—or his football?

Thank you for this opportunity to present my views.

Statement of Charles M. Neinas, Executive Director of the College Football Association

My name is Charles Neinas and I am the executive director of the College Football Association. The CFA is comprised of 67 universities that are classified in NCAA Division I-A which designates the most competitive classification in the sport of football. The CFA was founded in

1977 to provide a forum for universities to address subjects that are of particular interest to those involved in what is termed major college football. The CFA encourages the chief executive officers, faculty representatives, athletics directors and football coaches to work together on a common agenda. Through the years, the CFA has been in the forefront in strengthening academic standards, establishing restrictive rules governing recruiting and in the promotion of college football.

The Board of Directors of the CFA (roster attached) is most appreciative of the committee's willingness to consider what impact Title IX and the activities of the Office for Civil Rights (OCR) have upon college athletics. While created to consider matters related to major college football, our interest extends to college football at all levels as well as intercollegiate athletics for both men and women.

My primary mission today is to encourage continued congressional review of Title IX and to analyze the appropriateness of the interpretations and regulations that were adopted 20 years ago. In view of the changing landscape of intercollegiate athletics and the continuing progress that has been made in the development and growth of women's sports, there should be consideration as to whether the guidelines and Policy Interpretations of OCR reflect the current state of intercollegiate athletics.

For the record, let me state the following:

(1) We DO NOT seek repeal of Title IX.
(2) We DO NOT seek changes that would hinder the development of women's athletics.
(3) We DO NOT seek exemption of football from Title IX.
(4) We DO seek practical and reasonable interpretations and guidelines from OCR to eliminate colleges and universities from becoming prisoners to a strict proportionality test.

OCR established three tests in determining compliance with Title IX: proportionality, history of development and interest and abilities. Although OCR repeats that it utilizes the three tests in determining compliance, it is apparent by its actions that OCR considers the history of development and the interests and abilities tests as intermediate measures in reaching proportionality.

We believe that the unique size of college football teams needs to be taken into consideration as the Office for Civil Rights Policy Interpretations of 1979 promised.

At several institutions, intercollegiate football is *unique* among sports. The *size* of the teams, the expense of the operation, and the revenue produced distinguish football from other sports, both men's and women's. Title IX requires that "an institution must comply with the prohibition against sex discrimination imposed by that title and its implementing regulations in the administration of any revenue producing intercollegiate athletic activity." However, the unique size and cost of football programs have been taken into account in developing the Policy Interpretations (Policy Interpretations, Section IX, Appendix A, paragraph 5, 71419).

Clearly, football was intended to be covered by Title IX, and the cost of certain aspects is what the Javits Amendment required as sex neutral considerations; i.e., the fact that football would cost more is not discriminatory. However, the unique size of college football teams is not taken into consideration by the Policy Interpretations, and the result is that current interpretations by OCR and the courts in imposing strict proportionality is narrow and unworkable. . . .

At one time the number of sports offered men at a university far exceeded the sports offerings for women. This is no longer true! At many institutions the number of sports for women are equal to or greater than the number of sports offered for men.

Also, it is not true that the overall growth of women's programs has not been at the expense of men's sports. Universities have had to accommodate the need to expand programs and increase opportunities for women and in so doing eliminated men's sports for a variety of reasons. For example, during the past ten years, 64 NCAA members have discontinued men's swimming. Over the last 20 years, the number of wrestling programs in the NCAA has been reduced from 401 to 261. A survey of CFA members indicates that in the last ten years there have been 123 sports added for women and 39 sports for men have been discontinued.

Perhaps the greatest fallacy of all lies in the assertion that the unique size of college football programs was taken into account in the development of the Policy Interpretations. As discussed earlier, this simply is not true. Another problem with the Policy Interpretations is that it makes no distinction between the different division levels. While the I-A and I-AA distinctions are for the sport of football, most institutions competing at each level have different funding sources. Many of the Division I-A institutions have fully funded women's programs that benefit tremendously from the existence of football and the revenue that is generated through gate receipts, television and donors to the athletic program whose primary interest is college football. Those universities where football teams compete at the I-AA level do not have the same funding resources but also do not have as many scholarships or coaches. These institutions depend heavily on financial contributions from alumni and fund raising to support their intercollegiate teams because they do not enjoy the same level of attendance or interest.

The problem of strict proportionality impacts upon all institutions sponsoring the sport of football whether it be at the Division I-A level or Division III. Footballs, helmets and shoulder pads cost the same whether you are buying equipment for the University of Nebraska or Central College of Pella, Iowa. The Nebraskas, Penn States and Notre Dames of the world will continue to sponsor football because it is the primary source of income that funds the entire athletic program and also serves as a public relations and fund raising instrument for the university as a whole. Other men's sports at such institutions, however, may suffer as a result. It is when you talk about those programs sponsored at the Division II and the Division III level of the NCAA that football is in jeopardy of being discontinued.

There are two indisputable facts when comparing participation rates between men's and women's sports. First, football *requires and attracts* a larger number of participants. The overall average squad size in the sport of football ranges from 117 at the Division I-A level to 77 at the Division III level. Second, more men are interested in participating in intercollegiate athletics than women, even though at the Division I level there is more financial aid available per capita and absolute dollars for the women in matched sports. An analysis of the 1993–1994 participation study by the NCAA illustrates the point. Comparing like sports at the Division I level (basketball, cross country, fencing, golf, gymnastics, lacrosse, skiing, soccer, swimming, tennis, track and field [both indoor and outdoor], volleyball, crew and squash), men's participation average total is 347.9 and the women's participation average is 274.6. Yet more grants are available to women in these sports than to men. Nonetheless, men represent 56 percent of the participants and women represent 44 percent. Would this meet the strict proportionality test if a student body was 50 percent male and 50 percent female? It is even more onerous if the female student body is greater than 50 percent. It definitely would not meet OCR's compliance test and demonstrates the absurdity of strict proportionality.

Let us cite a specific example. The University of North Carolina at Chapel Hill was awarded last year's Sears Director's Cup that recognizes an institution's athletic achievement by combining the success of its men's and women's sports programs. The University of North Carolina at Chapel Hill currently has an enrollment of 42 percent male and 58 percent female. It sponsors 13 sports for women and will add a fourteenth sport for women next year. Women's sports do not lack for funding at the University of North Carolina. The institution also sponsors 13 sports for men. The participation rate in the athletic department, however, is almost the reverse of the gender enrollment of the student body with more than 50 percent of the participants being male. Who is to say that the University of North Carolina is not providing adequate competitive opportunities for all students on the campus, both male and female?

Some advocates of women's athletics have stated publicly that a method to achieve strict proportionality would be to reduce opportunities for men. They would eliminate those that wish to try out for a team, what we refer to as walk-ons. Because women do not try out in the same numbers their ill-founded solution is to eliminate opportunities for men and that is not the American way. Many of those that walk on do not make the final squad. Some, however, become outstanding athletes and major contributors to the university, as many coaches will testify.

Let us consider proportionality at the Division III level. Central College of Pella, Iowa has long had a successful football program. Central College is proud of the fact that of a student enrollment of 1,400, of which approximately 55 percent is female, there are 125 members on the football squad. At the Division III level, those that are attending college pay their own way. There are no athletic grants-in-aid. The reason that they are on the football squad is that they want an opportunity to play the game. Should Central College be required to limit the number that want to play football because of a strict proportionality test?

Those who attack football concentrate primarily on those institutions that sponsor the sport at the highest competitive level, Division I-A. In so doing, they question the need for a specific number of grants-in-aid with the expectation that if such numbers were reduced, the money should automatically go to support women's sports. This attack is unfair, unfounded and not in the best interest of women's sports. Look at the current Sears Director's Cup standings that reflect institutions having achieved success in athletics for both men and women. Without exception the highest rated programs are associated with universities that also sponsor football at the Division I-A level. The fact is that the most prominent and best funded women's athletic programs benefit because those universities also sponsor major college football. That fact should demonstrate above all else that football, despite its size and because of its popularity, does aid women's sports.

I find it difficult to believe that the sponsors of Title IX, in their desire to promote opportunities for women's education, including athletics, intended to hurt football or eliminate opportunities for men. Although Title IX is an educational act, the focus on strict proportionality rests solely on athletics and there is no investigation about the percentage of females enrolled in business or engineering or males enrolled in nursing or education. In fact, Senator Bayh, the Senate sponsor of Title IX, is quoted from the Congressional Record August 6, 1971 as stating, "What we are trying to do is to provide *equal access* for women and men students to the educational process and the extracurricular activities in a school, where there is not a unique facet such as football involved."

Let me reiterate what I said earlier:

(1) We are not asking football to be exempt from Title IX.

(2) The unique size of the sport of football must be taken into consideration. This is what the Policy Interpretations promised but failed to deliver.

(3) If participation in sports is good for men, it must also be good for women. Hopefully, there will be opportunities available to both.

(4) We seek practical interpretations and guidelines relative to Title IX. The current Policy Interpretation needs to be revisited because it is outdated and lacks the necessary clarification by the agency that is responsible to interpret it . . . OCR.

Finally, do not make those colleges and universities that sponsor football prisoners of strict proportionality.

17

ANGIE WATTS

High School Athletes Talk about Gender Equity
1998

In 1998, Washington Post staff writer Angie Watts sat down with four male high school athletes from the southern Maryland area and asked them for their candid thoughts about girls' sports and gender equity. The next week she did the same with three female high school athletes. Only half in jest, Watts characterized the tenor of the boys' comments as being along the lines of "you throw like a girl," to which the girls replied, "I may throw like a girl, but I can throw a heck of a lot faster, farther, and finer than most boys." While varsity athletics for girls is now an established part of high school life, it still has a long way to go in terms of earning equal resources and respect.

The participants, and their varsity sports:

> *Anthony King (football, basketball, track)*
> *Travis Mister (basketball, baseball)*
> *Daunte Neal (football, wrestling)*
> *Nick Vitielliss (basketball, baseball)*
> *Cindy Livesay (volleyball, softball)*
> *Beth White (volleyball, softball)*
> *Dawn Wood (field hockey, softball, track)*

The Male Athletes Speak

Do girls sports at your high schools receive the same amount of support—from fans, administrators, etc.—as the boys sports?

Daunte Neal: No, they don't. No one wants to see them.
Anthony King: No, because like during this season, football pulls in the most money. So, if football is pulling in the most money, nobody's

Angie Watts, "Male Athletes: Girls' Games Viewed 'More Like a JV Sport'" (October 18, 1998) and "Despite Equality Law, Girls Say They Get Shortchanged" (October 25, 1998), *Washington Post* Southern Maryland Extra.

going to go see field hockey. A couple people may go see volleyball, but there's not really as much of a demand as for football.

Neal: People see them more like a JV sport. You have a varsity football game, more people go to varsity than to the JV. It's the same with the girls; it's just that they're girls. Nobody really goes to see them except their parents and stuff...and somebody who has a girl-friend on the team....

Is it fair that during basketball season, the girls get the 6 p.m. time slot and the boys get the "prime time" game at 8 p.m.

[Nick] *Vitielliss:* The guys game is what brings the spectators, I think. People want to see the guys game. Because after the girls game, like, no one is there during the girls game. Then, when the guys are warming up, the gym gets packed.

[Travis] *Mister:* If the guys played first, then after the guys game, the whole crowd would leave.

Neal: Well, they say "ladies first," so they should go first.

Mister: That was pretty good.

What do the girls need to do to draw more fans in any of the girls sports?

Neal: They need somebody that stands out. Somebody that people want to come see. If on the basketball team they had a girl who was 6-3 and was dunking, people would come to see that girl dunk the ball.

What if she was 6-3 and was an excellent player and didn't dunk the ball?

Neal: If she was crossing people up and making them fall down, then I'd still come see. But she'd have to be something special. But there's nobody that really stands out that much. Just a lot of people running around.

Is there equal promotion for boys sports and girls sports?

Mister: Yes, at our school they are. If we have a sign made by the cheerleaders or somebody, it usually has both sports, like softball and baseball, on the same sign.

King: Yeah, they usually have signs up in our school, too.

But is that enough? Is it enough to get you to go to a girls game?

King: It depends on what I have planned, if I have practice myself or work to do for school. But if someone asks me, "Will you please go to the game?" then, yeah, I'll go. But otherwise, I try and find something important to do. . . .

So what if there's a girl who wants to play on your high school baseball team?

Mister: If they prove that they can play, then to tell you the truth, I don't have a problem with it. If they go out there, and do the job they are supposed to do.

What about a girl who wants to play football?

Vitielliss: You have to protect her.

King: If she can prove she can play, then I have no problem with it. But the thing is, if she's going to play, the rules shouldn't change because she's a girl. You know, like you get a 15-yard penalty because you hit her too hard or something, that shouldn't apply. Because I'm going to play equally. I'm going to play like I'm going to play.

Neal: That's right, because if she ain't no good, you can just run over her and the crowd can't tell that she's a girl. So you run her over.

King: But if she runs you over, you just look pitiful. Everybody would say, "Ain't that Number 12? She's a girl. You got run over by a girl."

Neal: But you have to hit her. She'd be just like everyone else. If coach said, "Hit her," I'd hit her.

King: Me, I would think twice about hitting her hard, but if I had to do my job, then I would do my job. Then I'd help her up, just like I help everyone up that I hit.

Neal: I wouldn't help her up. I don't help anyone up. At our practice, if you run somebody over, you don't help them up. That's because they got run over and next time they learn not to get run over again. She'd get the same treatment as everybody else.

What if a girl wanted to wrestle?

Neal: Nah, that can't happen.

Mister: We had a girl at my school one time that wanted to wrestle.

Neal: No, wrestling is different. You have football, that's a team, baseball, that's a team, but wrestling, this is one on one. If I wrestled a girl weighing my same weight, I know I'm going to be stronger than her. She's not going to have a chance. She may be quicker than me, she can be as quick as she wants, but she's going to get snatched one time. It's different because people watching can see she's a girl, and a guy is going to say, "I can't lose to no girl," so he is going to do whatever it takes to win. If that includes hurting her, some people will do that.

King: If so many girls want to do it, then I think there should be girl wrestling.

Neal: My football coach said he wrestled a girl when he was in high school and he just destroyed her, had her nose bleeding and everything. He said he felt terrible because she was crying, but that's part of the game. But what if a guy goes out and wants to play field hockey, and runs all the girls over. They'd start hollering, "That's not fair." But there's not guys field hockey, so what? . . .

What about a girl on a boys team who gets hurt? Gets hit by a pitch or someone takes a cheap shot at her on the football field? How would you react.

Neal: I think I would act different than if they just hit a guy.

Mister: I may say something, but I wouldn't charge the mound or anything.

What would you say?

Vitielliss: "Go easy on that girl."

Mister: I guess if she proves that she can play, you're just going to accept that she got hit.

Neal: If she's in a play and she gets hit, okay. But if it was intentional and he didn't have to hit her, and a big guy just sees a little girl and runs her over, then you're going to have to talk trash and say something to him. But if it was a guy that got run over, we'd laugh at him. When he came to the sidelines, we'd say, "Man, you just got run over" and stuff like that—it's part of the sport.

King: But if it's a girl, it's different.

Neal: Yeah, that's just morals.

Vitielliss: If she got hit and was just laying there on the ground, crying, then I don't know. If they can take it like the guys . . . take the hit and just go to first base or whatever, then that would show that she can hang with everybody. I'm not saying a girl would do that, lay and cry on the ground, but if she does take it and run to first base like everybody else does, then that's just more respect for her.

Mister: But it would be hard for a girl to be part of the team because they couldn't be in the locker room, be a part of that. Before practice and after practice, that's where you build team chemistry....

The Female Athletes Speak

Do girls sports at your high schools receive the same amount of support—from fans, administrators, etc.—as the boys sports?

Cindy Livesay: When we go and ask for sponsors, more people want to go sponsor football or baseball, so they get more money. For volleyball or even softball, our fields, our scoreboards are smaller. They have, like, sprinklers out in the baseball field that come out, during winter they have that, and our field is just all dried out.

Dawn Wood: Since you reminded me of that... at our school, the baseball teams are getting two new fields, and what do the girls' softball teams get? We get the old baseball fields. How coincidental is it that they get the new fields while we get the old one, which is, of course, set up to be a baseball field, so they have to take out the mounds, and all of that. Everything is announced over the loudspeaker pretty evenly, but the posters? Always football. They always have the signs. The fans really care about varsity football. For field hockey and other girls sports, most of the time it's just parents or boyfriends who care.

What is the difference between the way boys and girls sports are handled by the schools?

Beth White: At football games they sell barbecue, barbecue chicken, hot dogs, hamburgers, and at volleyball or softball all they sell is candy bars.

Livesay: Our parents have to support the concession stands, the school doesn't support it. They do for football, but not for us.

Livesay: We have to do fund-raisers for new uniforms.

White: And football just gets new uniforms.... But to add on to the girls not getting as much publicity outside of high school, I was on the World Series team [Big League Softball] for two years, and we won. And our game, just our last game, was a delayed tape on ESPN2, and every single boys game was on Monday, Tuesday, Wednesday, Thursday, Friday....

What about the time slot for a basketball doubleheader? The boys said they think the girls should play in the earlier time because, if not, the fans would all walk out after the boys game was over. Do you think the girls basketball teams should sometimes get the later, 8 p.m. time slot?

Wood: They should at least rotate it.

White: I don't think, necessarily, the fans would get up and leave when the girls started warming up.

Livesay: Once they see the level of play, I think more fans would come.

The boys said they wouldn't come watch girls basketball anyway because they can't dunk.

White: I think that's a bunch of crap.

Wood: Actually, I don't know. Because I was watching one game in the WNBA, and that was enough for me. They missed so many shots. I was thinking, "Why am I even watching this?" I don't know if you guys play basketball or not, sorry, but when I watched it, they were awful. . . .

The question to the boys was if they had 5-year-old twins, a boy and a girl, would you encourage them equally to play sports? And the boys said they would push the boy harder. What about you?

White: I wouldn't make either of the kids play, but I would, like, persuade them into playing. If the girl didn't want to play like volleyball or softball, but wanted to cheerlead or dance, then I don't think I'd have a problem with that, because she still wants to do something. Even if the boy didn't want to play any sports or anything, I would want him to do something, some activity, but I wouldn't push him into sports.

Livesay: I think most men do want to force their sons into sports because of the stereotypes if they don't stay active. There are a lot of stereotypes about guys. Like if they are not an athlete, then they are not a man.

Would you push a daughter the same way?

Livesay: Definitely, because I think they would grow up to be a better human being, really. Kids are better students in school when they stay active.

White: If I have kids, then as long as they are being active and staying in school and not getting into trouble, then I don't think I'd have a problem if they weren't playing a varsity sport.

Livesay: As long as they are using their time wisely. . . .

What about having boys play on girls sports teams?

Wood: I think if we had boys on girls sports teams it would be more competitive. At least I think so, because the girls would want to show the boys up.

White: Yeah. I think it would be more competitive between the girls and the guys because they would want to do better than one another.

Livesay: But that would be being more competitive between your own teammates than with the other team. The boys would think we're too delicate and too soft.

White: Yeah, because we have issues.

Everyone: [Laughter].

White: I don't think guys take girls sports seriously.

Wood: They don't take the time to understand them before they think they can play them.

White: I think some boys say they consider girls sports more like a JV sport because they go to watch varsity football over varsity volleyball. Or even during the spring, they'll go watch varsity baseball over varsity softball. If they would just come and watch us, I think they would want to watch us more. But they won't give us the time of day.

Wood: Like my boyfriend, who has never played field hockey, never touched a stick, and I've been playing for five years, he expected to be just as good as me. He was going to teach me how to play lacrosse one day, so I said I'd teach him how to play field hockey. So we were out in the front yard and we were going one on one and he gets so mad because I was dodging around him. He said, "Man, I can never hit the ball." And I said, "Well what do you expect? It's your first day. Do you expect to just be able to come out there and be on the same level with me?" If he was on the same level with me in one day, then I am doing something wrong.

Should girls be able to play on boys teams? Should they be able to play football, or wrestle?

White: If they wanted to, yeah.

Wood: But one year we did have a girl football player, and she thought she was special. Thought she should have special rules, like, "You can't tackle me."

White: I don't think that would be fair. There shouldn't be any special rules.

Wood: If you want to play with the boys, then you better just play.

Livesay: You can't go in there thinking you are special. You have to blend in.

The boys said that if a girl came out for their team they would just be harder on her to see if she could take it.

Livesay: I could see that. They'd want to outdo her, want to beat her.

Wood: Because, like they said, it would look bad for them if they lost to a girl.

White: Or in football, if they got hit by a girl. Like they said, everyone would know No. 12 or whoever was a girl. And it would be "ha, ha, ha." And like Daunte [Neal] said, he would just knock her down and not help her up, even if she was crying. That's a bunch of crap. I watch football games and they all help each other up. . . .

What about the level of competition of girls sports in high schools? Is there as big a push to have a winning girls program as there is to have a winning football program?

Wood: To our coaches it is, it's just as important to win. But when you look at it as an overall thing, I think they are more worried about the boys sports winning than the girls.

White: I don't think students look at volleyball or softball or field hockey as being as important as football, so they don't really care if we win.

If a local football team won a state title, what do you think the reaction would be?

Wood: Oh, my God, the school would go crazy.

White: Okay, the perfect example. My sophomore year, our football team went to the playoffs and they got coach buses, they got let out of school early, they went to the principal's office and got dough-nuts and drinks and stuff. And we went to the state playoffs last year for volleyball, and we got a congratulations from our principal. . . .

What are the biggest differences in high school between boys and girls sports?

Livesay: The number of fans and the publicity that the boys get.

Wood: Also the fields and the equipment.

White: The money and the equipment. Football gets new uniforms and new equipment and so many things offered to buy because people have to pay money to get in and watch them, so they bring the most money in. Whereas you don't have to pay to watch softball, so we're not bringing any money in to get new equipment.

It is a fact that football brings in the most money. Is it fair then, in your minds, that since they are bringing in the money they should get to benefit from that?

White: Well, with people not having to pay to come watch us, it's like criticizing us. Saying we're not good enough that people would come pay to see us. And with the money from concessions and stuff, it's not just the football parents who are working that, it's the athletic boosters.

How do you think girls sports should be viewed?

Livesay: I think the boys were basing their view just from stereotypes on girls, like how they are so feminine and delicate and sweet, but nowadays we are more athletic, and we are a lot stronger than we appear.

White: We are also more competitive. We've come a long way in sports. Boys have always been big in sports, but girls are moving up—and it's just like the same. . . . When guys come to watch us play, they're like, "How do you pitch like that?" And they are really impressed . . . when they come to watch. But if they never come to watch, they'd just be like, "Oh, it's a girls sport."

Wood: We're still seen as the weaker of the two sexes. But if some of the guys would actually open their eyes and come and watch us, they may not agree with that anymore. Even though it's proven that male bodies are stronger than females', let me tell you what: There's some of those boys—I'm telling you, I could knock them over.

18

JESSICA GAVORA

A Conservative Critique of Title IX
2002

In Tilting the Playing Field: Schools, Sports, Sex and Title IX *(2002), Jessica Gavora laments the fact that so many of women's recent breakthroughs in sports are attributed to Title IX, rather than the hard work and accomplishment of the individual athletes themselves. Sharply critical of gender-equity policies that diminish opportunities for men in the name of opening such opportunities for women, she questions whether women and girls really are identical in their interests to boys and men. Gavora's critique of Title IX is really a critique of many of the priorities of the modern feminist movement.*

In 1972, I was an awkward, outsized fourth-grader, pushing six feet tall. Boys had little use for me, and I was an uninspired student. What saved me was sports.

Basketball, to be exact. I could catch a basketball with one hand (the ability to "palm" the ball would come a year later, in fifth grade). Basketball was what I could do—what I thought I was *meant* to do. My brother Rudy and I played hours of one-on-one underneath the hoop in front of our house in Fairbanks, Alaska. Rudy was bigger and older than I was, but I still occasionally managed to inspire a breathless "nice shot!" from him. And I learned a lot from the competition he provided. So when the opportunity came along to play "organized" ball at Joy Elementary School in 1972, I grabbed it.

If you've ever seen fourth-grade girls play basketball, you know there was actually nothing organized about our game. Turnovers were constant, the refs couldn't keep up with the fouls and calls for traveling, and dramatic fast breaks were often mistakenly scored at the team's own basket. Still, my girlfriends and I took basketball seriously

---

Jessica Gavora, *Tilting the Playing Field: Schools, Sports, Sex and Title IX* (San Francisco: Encounter Books, 2002), 1–2, 4–5, 8–9.

and spent our precious recesses practicing in the gym while the rest of our classmates took to the swings and monkey bars outside.

We had no idea (nor, I suspect, did our teachers) that a law had just been passed in Washington, D.C.—still a long way from Fairbanks back in 1972—guaranteeing the right of fourth-grade girls to play basketball. Perhaps it was just something to do during those long Alaskan winters; but whatever the reason, I was blessed that year to begin an athletic career that enriched my life in ways I am only now beginning to realize.

I played basketball devotedly, fanatically, every year for the next nine years. Although my sports career never went beyond high school, it taught me invaluable lessons for successful adulthood: How to push myself hard—and go farther than I ever thought I could. How to be magnanimous in success and dignified in failure. How to work as part of a team. How to keep enjoying the benefits of physical fitness long after the effortless energy of youth is gone.

Now that I have grown up, lost my inside game and become an occasional critic of contemporary feminism, I am often approached by people (usually women) who remind me that I, like other young American women, stand on the shoulders of earlier generations of feminists. I am told that the kinds of opportunities I had at Joy Elementary School were not guaranteed but won by the sacrifices of women who went before me. And I take these admonitions seriously. In fact, I am grateful to have grown up in a country and at a time when my interests and ambitions, however much against the grain, were supported and encouraged. I would not have been happy in a world that forced me to be a dancer or a cheerleader when I really wanted to play basketball; nor would I want my own daughter to inherit such a world.

Like other women my age and younger, I grew up with an almost limitless sense of opportunity. Yet I have become aware that the women's movement we inherited, though claiming to support our liberation, fails to share our optimism and confidence. Instead of reflecting and, indeed, reveling in our expanded horizons, the feminism of the National Organization for Women and other so-called "women's groups" is oddly suspicious of our experience. It depicts women as passive victims rather than the makers of their own destinies, and overlooks our individuality in favor of a collective political identity that many of us find restrictive. . . .

The phrase "unintended consequences" is a familiar one in the debate over the excesses of the modern bureaucratic state. Typically it is invoked to explain why a well-intended government program or policy has somehow gone terribly awry—for example, how a policy of open-ended, no-questions-asked welfare benefits encouraged illegitimacy and dependence. But perhaps nowhere in the litany of second thoughts about the nanny state are "unintended consequences" invoked more often than in reference to Title IX. To be exact, a law designed to end discrimination against women is now causing discrimination against men.

The dictates of gender politics are such that the brave public official who dares to utter a negative word about Title IX must be careful to confine his or her criticism to its "unintended consequences." These artfully worded statements often begin with sweeping tributes to the law and the progress it has ostensibly yielded for women. Only later—in suddenly small, halting voices—do the critics express qualms about the law's application. Title IX should not be implemented as a "quota law," they say. Quotas are bad, as even the most radical practitioner of identity politics acknowledges. Quotas are also the squid's ink of any discussion of race or gender, the term whose mere mention clouds the issue in such a way that the advocate of preferences gets away with his or her commitment intact. Of course we are all against quotas!

And so the preponderance of what the public hears about Title IX today focuses on the positive, the heroic, the groundbreaking. It seems that a woman cannot be successful in athletics without that success being attributed not to her talent and dedication, but to a federal law. Thus the members of the U.S. Women's World Cup soccer team, who won a stunning victory over China in 1999, are "the daughters of Title IX." Likewise, Sheryl Swoopes, Kym Hampton, Rebecca Lobo and the other stars of the Women's National Basketball Association are not merely great athletes and fierce competitors, but also the embodiment of the beneficiaries of a federal law. The fact that portraying these remarkable athletes as creatures of entitlement—the welfare queens of the sports world—diminishes their achievement never seems to occur to those feminists who use them for a political agenda.

Still, these efforts to tie all women's athletic achievement to Title IX find a receptive audience in the proud moms and dads of multiplying hordes of pigtailed soccer players today—especially the dads, who are now just as able to live vicariously through their daughters' athletic exploits as those of their sons. To them, giving these energetic, bright-eyed little competitors an equal chance to kick a ball or swing a bat is an unassailable good, one that is beyond question in polite society. . . .

But why, it might be asked, should any of this Title IX business worry us at all? Girls and women suffered centuries of discrimination and lack of opportunity, so isn't it a good thing that they now have a leg up in our schools and universities? And don't we have an obligation to protect our gains, to guard against backsliding, and to ferret out discrimination and restrictions on opportunity where they remain?

As Christina Hoff Sommers noted in the opening pages of her seminal book *Who Stole Feminism?* American women do indeed owe a great debt to those leaders of the women's movement who fought to break down barriers to the full and equal participation of women in American life. That we have not only won these opportunities but also taken full advantage of them to realize our potential as women has been good—not just for individual women but for workplaces, communities and families.

That being said, it must also be remembered that the contemporary women's movement is now entering its fifth decade. A baby girl born the year Title IX was passed will be thirty this year. She grew up in a country where her rights were protected and, more importantly, she came of age in a society where her equality was overwhelmingly accepted and respected. She and the other women born in 1972 are now the parents, teachers, coaches, professors and administrators who control our educational institutions. In short, they are full participants in the "system" that Title IX feminists still assert is routinely and systematically victimizing them.

The current interpretation of Title IX, I will argue, is at odds with the experience of the women who have grown up since the law was passed. Questioning its wisdom is of a piece with questions raised in the last decade by Sommers and others about the relevance of the modern feminist movement to the vast majority of American women. Do the activists who are leading the fight for Title IX quotas really represent the grievances, wishes and aspirations of the majority of American women? Are girls and women really, as the law has been twisted to assume, identical in their interests and abilities to boys and men? Are we as likely to want to kick a ball or take a physics class? Should the law penalize men if we are not?

Questioning what has come to be known as the struggle for "gender equity" is considered sex treason by the hardcore feminists who dominate the women's movement. But I believe that women should welcome a close scrutiny of this gender obsession and what it is bringing to sports and education. And not just because boys and men—our sons and husbands and brothers—are finding themselves on the losing end of a federal regulatory regime that now officially prefers women, although that occurs with depressing regularity. What should be of greater concern to those who care about equal opportunity for girls and women is the implicit message of Title IX today: that young girls aren't worthy of respect and admiration unless and until they act like young boys. Playing sports and studying the hard sciences, those who enforce the law tell us, are worthier than the interests women have traditionally pursued. And to make sure no one misses the point, this message is backed up by real advantages in funding and resource allocation for girls and women who act accordingly—and by just as real penalties for boys and men. The losers aren't just males but also the millions of females whose talents and interests lie outside those dictated by the affirmative androgyny of the law.

Title IX and American Culture

19

DONNA LOPIANO

A Women-Centered View of Sport
1986

When the National Collegiate Athletic Association won control over women's athletics from the Association for Intercollegiate Athletics for Women in 1982, many wondered how women's sports might change. Donna Lopiano, a former athlete and then athletic administrator at the University of Texas at Austin, had an honest answer: "I don't know." She did, however, have a vision of what "women-centered or feminist sport" might look like, of which the following is an excerpt. It is both a critique of the prevailing male-centered values of sport and a call for an alternative approach that emphasizes sport as a means of self-knowledge and personal discovery of benefit to both men and women.

1. *All men and women should have the opportunity to explore their physical selves*, to test their abilities and limits over the broadest range and levels of self-chosen physical activities.
2. Sport should be a "means" by which one gets to know oneself, not an end in and of itself. The participant exploits the

Donna Lopiano, "A Political Analysis of the Possibility of Impact Alternatives for the Accomplishment of Feminist Objectives within American Intercollegiate Sport," in Richard E. Lapchick, *Fractured Focus: Sport as a Reflection of Society* (Lexington, Mass.: D. C. Heath, 1986). The original version was presented at the 1982 Women as Leaders in Physical Education Workshop at the University of Iowa.

possibilities of sport, not vice versa. That does not mean that *sport* cannot be exploited, but I am saying that participants *must* not be exploited.

3. The participant's access to the knowledge and ultimate possibilities of sport—their exposure to coaches, their use of sporting equipment, their ability to compete against those of equal or greater skill—should not be limited by gender or race or socio-economic class distinctions. If this appears to be a simple explanation, it is. Sport involves nothing more than propelling an object through space or overcoming the resistance of a mass with various measures of performance (time, distance, accuracy, efficiency, weight or qualitative estimates of grace or aesthetic values) being used to evaluate progress or levels of achievement. The performer, the spectator, the coach and various other actors or observers bring their own values to a quintessentially meaningless human activity.

Access to a self-chosen sport activity is one problem, one item on the feminist agenda. It will always be a constant problem. The other side of the coin, the second and more critical problem is the primacy of the feminist value system which should be attached to sport. I have defined that value as allowing the *individual* to know his or her physical self in terms of strength, speed, reaction time and, depending on the context of performance, his or her physiological and psychological response to physical stress and to others who are also participating as integral or ancillary elements of the sport experience. Men and women *value* the opportunity to know themselves in such ways. Let me suggest to you that these so-called "feminist" values are inherent in the nature of sport—a given. They are simply not emphasized as primary or most important.

As with most important human pursuits, activities like sport which are valued, have a tendency to become institutionalized, to become highly organized within a social system. They then attract an overlay of values which are important to the society as a whole. It is a given that society's dominant public institutions will inevitably seek to exploit any human activity which is valued—to make money, to retain power, to exercise power over others. No feminist agenda can realistically overcome that cement-encased reality of societal tendency. There will be a constant pull or struggle for the primacy of values between those preferred by the individual and those preferred by the larger society in which the individual exists.

The only alternative therefore, the task before us, is to focus the feminist agenda on allowing the participant to retain control over the meaning of sport to him and her, to retain the primacy of the self-knowledge values and thus resist the exploitive tendencies of the society-at-large.

As another sidelight, I would suggest to you that the fact that much of American amateur sport resides in the institution of education creates a unique leverage. Our society has permitted education in general and higher education in particular to have a degree of license not tolerated in law, politics or economics, to have a vastly different value primacy in many instances. Therefore, sport in education can be a very practical and potentially more profitable focus for feminist intentions.

So let me add a #4 to our description of women-centered feminist sport:

4. The retention of an athlete's right to resist and prevent participant exploitation.

20

JAMES L. SHULMAN AND WILLIAM G. BOWEN

Female Athletes and the Game of Life

2001

In their influential study The Game of Life: College Sports and Educational Values *(2001), James L. Shulman and William G. Bowen documented the growing gap between an increasingly commercialized and competitive sports culture on the nation's campuses and the educational values and priorities of those same institutions. Analyzing data from cohorts of students entering thirty colleges and universities in 1951, 1976, 1989, and 1999, they confirmed that in the years since Title IX has been in effect, the experiences of female athletes have increasingly replicated those of the dominant male athletic model, including lower*

James L. Shulman and William G. Bowen, *The Game of Life: College Sports and Educational Values* (Princeton, N.J.: Princeton University Press, 2001), 258–63, 264–65.

SAT scores at admission and lower academic standing once enrolled, and that this convergence will likely continue. Whether women athletes will receive long-term rewards commensurate with those which men reap—"increased self-confidence, the applause of growing numbers of fans, and post-college networks that support them as they move from the playing fields to the trading desks"[1]*—remains an open question.*

Scale: Numbers of Athletes and Athletic Recruitment

1. *Athletes competing on intercollegiate teams constitute a sizable share of the undergraduate student population at many selective colleges and universities, and especially at coed liberal arts colleges and Ivy League universities.* In 1989, intercollegiate athletes accounted for nearly one-third of the men and approximately one-fifth of the women who entered the coed liberal arts colleges participating in this study; male and female athletes accounted for much smaller percentages of the entering classes in the Division IA scholarship schools, which of course have far larger enrollments; the Ivies are intermediate in the relative number of athletes enrolled, with approximately one-quarter of the men and 15 percent of the women playing on intercollegiate teams. Some of the much larger Division IA schools, public and private, enrolled a smaller absolute number of athletes than either the more athletically oriented coed liberal arts colleges or the Ivies—primarily because a number of the Division IA schools sponsor fewer teams.

2. *The relative number of male athletes in a class has not changed dramatically over the past 40 years, but athletes in recent classes have been far more intensely recruited than used to be the case.* This statement holds for the coed liberal arts colleges as well as the universities. In 1989, roughly 90 percent of the men who played the High Profile sports of football, basketball, and hockey said that they had been recruited (the range was from 97 percent in the Division IA public universities to 83 percent in the Division III coed liberal arts colleges), and roughly two-thirds of the men who competed in other sports such as tennis, soccer, and swimming said that they too had been recruited. In the '76 cohort, these percentages were much lower; there were many more "walk-ons" in 1976 than in 1989, and there were surely fewer still in the most recent entering classes.

[1]Shulman and Bowen, *The Game of Life*, 180.

3. *Only tiny numbers of women athletes in the '76 entering cohort reported having been recruited, but that situation had changed markedly by the time of the '89 entering cohort; recruitment of women athletes at these schools has moved rapidly in the direction of the men's model.* Roughly half of the women in the '89 cohort who played intercollegiate sports in the Ivies and the Division IA universities reported that having been recruited by the athletic department played a significant role in their having chosen the schools they attended. The comparable percentages in the coed colleges and the women's colleges were much lower in '89, but women athletes at those schools are now also being actively recruited.

Admissions Advantages, Academic Qualifications, and Other "Selection" Effects

1. *Athletes who are recruited, and who end up on the carefully winnowed lists of desired candidates submitted by coaches to the admissions office, now enjoy a very substantial statistical "advantage" in the admissions process—a much greater advantage than that enjoyed by other targeted groups such as underrepresented minority students, alumni children, and other legacies; this statement is true for both male and female athletes.* At a representative non-scholarship school for which we have complete data on all applicants, recruited male athletes applying for admission to the '99 entering cohort had a 48 percent greater chance of being admitted than did male students at large, after taking differences in SAT scores into account; the corresponding admissions advantage enjoyed by recruited women athletes in '99 was 53 percent. The admissions advantages enjoyed by minority students and legacies were in the range of 18 to 24 percent.

2. *The admissions advantage enjoyed by men and women athletes at this school, which there is reason to believe is reasonably typical of schools of its type, was much greater in '99 than in '89, and it was greater in '89 than in '76.* The trend—the directional signal—is unmistakably clear.

3. *One obvious consequence of assigning such a high priority to admitting recruited athletes is that they enter these colleges and universities with considerably lower SAT scores than their classmates.* This pattern holds for both men and women athletes and is highly consistent by type of school. The SAT "deficit" is most pronounced for men and women who play sports at the Division IA schools, least pronounced for women at the liberal arts colleges (especially the women's colleges),

and middling at the Ivies. Among the men at every type of school, the SAT deficits are largest for those who play the High Profile sports of football, basketball, and hockey.

4. *Admitted athletes differ from their classmates in other ways too, and there is evidence of an "athlete culture."* In addition to having weaker academic qualifications, athletes who went on to play on intercollegiate teams were clearly different in other ways at the time they entered college. They were decidedly more competitive than students at large. The male athletes were also more interested than students at large in pursuing business careers and in achieving financial success (this is not true, however, of the women athletes); athletes placed considerably less emphasis on the goals of making original contributions to science or the arts. The differences between athletes and their classmates along many of these dimensions have widened with the passage of time. In addition, athletes who compete in the Lower Profile sports (such as track, swimming, lacrosse, and tennis) had begun, by the time of the '89 cohort, to share more of the attributes of the athlete culture that earlier were found mostly among the High Profile athletes. Similarly, whereas women athletes in the '76 cohort were largely indistinguishable from their classmates in most respects, by the time of the '89 cohort women who played sports had more and more in common with the male athletes (for example, entering college with both lower standardized test scores and more politically conservative views than other women students).

5. *Contrary to much popular mythology, recruitment of athletes has no marked effect on either the socioeconomic composition of these schools or in their racial diversity.* Male athletes (especially those who play High Profile sports at the Division IA schools) are more likely than students at large to come from modest socioeconomic backgrounds and to be African Americans. Nonetheless, elimination of the athletic contribution to racial diversity in the '89 cohort would have caused the percentage of African American men enrolled at these schools to decline by just 1 percentage point—an estimate obtained by recalculating the percentage of African American students who would have been enrolled had the racial mix of athletes been the same as the racial mix of students at large. There would even be an opposite effect among the women, since the share of African American women playing college sports is much lower—often half the corresponding percentage—of African American women students at large. Moreover, until very recently, women athletes were more likely than other

women students to come from privileged backgrounds. Those men who play Lower Profile sports continue to come from more advantaged backgrounds than either the other athletes or the rest of their male classmates.

Graduation Rates, Underperformance in the Classroom, and Choice of Major

1. *Despite their lower SATs, athletes who attended the selective schools included in this study, along with their classmates who participated in other time-intensive extracurricular activities, graduated at very high rates.* The national problem of low graduation rates—which has attracted the attention of both the NCAA and the public—does not afflict most athletes or other students who attend these schools.

2. *When we examine grades (rank-in-class), an entirely different picture emerges: the academic standing of athletes, relative to that of their classmates, has deteriorated markedly in recent years.* Whereas male athletes in the '51 cohort were slightly more likely than other students to be in the top third of their class, only 16 percent of those in the '89 cohort finished in the top third, and 58 percent finished in the bottom third. Women athletes in the '76 cohort did as well academically as other women, but women athletes in the '89 cohort were more likely than other women to be in the bottom third of the class. This pattern is especially pronounced in those sets of schools where women athletes were highly recruited; the women's colleges are alone in showing no gap at all in academic performance between women athletes and other women students in the '89 cohort.

3. *Only part of this decline in the academic performance of athletes can be attributed to their lower levels of aptitude or preparation at the time they began college; they consistently underperform academically even after we control for differences in standardized test scores and other variables.* Academic underperformance among athletes is a pervasive phenomenon. In the '89 cohort, it is found among both male and female athletes and among those who played all types of sports (not just among the men who played football, basketball, and hockey); it is more pronounced within the Ivy League and the coed liberal arts colleges than it is within the Division IA schools.

4. *Academic underperformance in college has roots in high school academic performance in the priority assigned by athletes to academics, and in the "culture of sport."* The degree of underperformance varies

not only with pre-college academic indicators, but also with how many other athletes who played on the same terms underperformed (possible peer effects) and whether athletes cited a coach as a principal mentor. The "culture of sport" interpretation of this pattern is supported by evidence showing that students who were active in other time-intensive extracurricular activities *overperformed* academically, relative to their SAT scores and other predictors.

5. *Male athletes have become highly concentrated in certain fields of study, especially the social sciences, and female athletes have started to show different patterns of majors as well.* At one Ivy League university, 54 percent of all High Profile athletes majored in economics or political science as compared with 18 percent of male students at large. When considered in the light of differences in career and financial goals, many of the choices of field of study by male athletes seem to be driven by a desire for something akin to a business major. More generally, this evidence on academic concentrations is consistent with other data on rooming patterns in suggesting a greatly increased tendency for athletes to band together. In the 1950s, male athletes were much more broadly distributed across fields of study and, in general, were more like their classmates in all respects.

21

WOMEN'S SPORTS FOUNDATION

Title IX and Race in Intercollegiate Sport
2003

Because some of the most dramatic (and publicized) breakthroughs in the 1990s came in sports in which women athletes of color are underrepresented, such as soccer, Title IX is sometimes accused of having mainly benefited "white-girl sports." To test that proposition, as well as the belief that male athletes of color have been hurt as general opportunities for

Women's Sports Foundation, "Title IX and Race in Intercollegiate Sport" (East Meadow, N.Y.: Women's Sports Foundation, 2003).

women increase, the Women's Sports Foundation commissioned a study. Its findings, presented here in its executive summary, document that sex discrimination affects all female athletes, with female athletes of color bearing an additional burden because of their race. The report also documents a strong pattern of racial inequality for men and women in specific sports, with the highest participation rates in established sports such as basketball and track and the lowest in emerging sports such as ice hockey, skiing, and equestrian. In the end, however, the report concludes that female athletes of color have experienced a dramatic increase in sports participation opportunities, an increase not at the expense of men, in the years since the passage of Title IX.

Executive Summary

Are women of color receiving their fair share of the opportunities in intercollegiate athletics? Some writers have suggested that female athletes of color have not accrued as many gains during the Title IX era of American sport as white female athletes. Other writers suggest that Title IX has hurt male athletes of color. Overall Title IX of the Education Amendments of 1972, the federal law that prohibits discrimination on the basis of sex in all education programs and activities receiving federal funds, has helped to spur girls' and women's participation in sport. Yet the assessment of progress in intercollegiate sport by women of color and men of color is confounded not only by the complexity of race relations in American history, but also by the scarcity of reliable data on minority athletic participation rates during the Title IX era (from 1970 to the present). Historically, both race and sex discrimination have shaped the patterns of institutional opportunity in sport and higher education. Thus, . . . untangling and understanding these forces is a complicated challenge.

The main purpose of this study was to examine the limited amount of available data on male and female athletes of color in collegiate sport in order to evaluate the extent to which their participation and scholarship support compares to those of white male and female athletes. We also attempted to measure or judiciously estimate some racial and gender trends in athletic participation since 1972, the year that Title IX became law. Whenever possible, we used NCAA data on athletic participation and graduation rates by gender and race, and United States Census Bureau statistics as the empirical basis for analysis.

THE ANALYSIS OF AVAILABLE EVIDENCE YIELDED
TEN MAJOR CONCLUSIONS

1. *Since the passage of Title IX, female college athletes of color have experienced a dramatic increase in NCAA sports participation opportunities.* For female athletes of color, there was a 955% increase in participation opportunities from 1971 to 2000 (2,137 to 22,541 participants respectively).

2. *Female college athletes of color have also experienced a substantial increase in scholarship assistance.* Women athletes of color received approximately $82 million in scholarship assistance in 1999 compared to less than $100,000 in 1971.

3. *Sex discrimination negatively impacts all female athletes, including female athletes of color.* Compared with the percentage of women of color enrolled at NCAA institutions (24.9% of female students), female athletes of color were underrepresented (14.8% of female students). A similar pattern of disproportionate representation existed for all female athletes (54.7% of all students enrolled, but only 42.1% of athletes were women).

4. *Unlike female athletes of color, male athletes of color in NCAA varsity sports (22.1% of male athletes) were proportionally represented compared to their presence in the student body (22% of male students).* However, the overrepresentation of male athletes of color in basketball and football, sports with high participation numbers, disguises a pattern of racial inequality in many other men's sports.

5. *There is a pattern of racial inequality in most NCAA sports.* This pattern of racial clustering appears to be related to continuing racism and the disparate impacts of economic inequality on populations of color. Clustering refers to a situation where athletes of color have very high participation rates in some sports but very low participation rates in others; e.g., male rates for athletes of color are very high in football but very low in swimming and diving. The analysis uncovered an overall pattern of underrepresentation of males of color in 14 of 25 intercollegiate sports and females of color in 20 of 25 intercollegiate sports in 2001. The realities of clustering must be addressed if male and female athletes of color are going to reap the same widespread athletic and educational benefits as their white counterparts.

6. *Sports help to advance opportunities for some students of color in higher education.* Male athletes of color in basketball (43%), football (34%), volleyball (29%), outdoor track (26%) and indoor track (24%) exceeded their overall student body representation (22%). Female ath-

letes of color in bowling (80%), badminton (33%) and basketball (29%) exceeded their overall student body representation (24.9%). However, in the sports of badminton and bowling for females, these sports reported extremely low rates of overall participation (33 and 197 total participants respectively).

7. *Scholarship opportunities for male and female athletes of color are greater than their proportion within the athlete population.* Male and female athletes of color were overrepresented among scholarship recipients (32.6% and 19.3%, respectively) compared to their representation in the total athlete population (26.4% and 17.5%, respectively). Male and female athletes of color also received a larger proportion of the scholarship dollars (36.2% and 19.5%, respectively) than would be expected considering their proportion in the total athlete populations (26.4% and 17.5%, respectively). However, female scholarship athletes of color (19.3%) were underrepresented in comparison to their proportion in the overall student body (26.2%).

8. *All female scholarship athletes graduated at higher rates than the general female student body.* Both white female scholarship athletes (68%) and female athletes of color who are on scholarship (55%) graduated at higher rates than their respective counterparts in the general student population (59% and 49%, respectively). White male scholarship athletes (53%) and male athletes of color (41%) who are on scholarship graduated at about the same rate as their respective general student counterparts (54% and 42%, respectively).

9. *Graduation rates of both female and male athletes of color were significantly lower than the corresponding rates for white athletes.* This relationship is also true for the general student body and demonstrates that regardless of athletic participation, students of color face unique challenges throughout their undergraduate educational experience.

10. *Title IX has not decreased the participation opportunities for male athletes of color.* More than 85% of the teams that have been discontinued (i.e., wrestling, tennis, gymnastics, rifle, and swimming) are in sports in which males of color are moderately or severely underrepresented. In addition, more than half of the total participation opportunities added for male athletes were in sports in which male athletes of color were overrepresented.

22

WELCH SUGGS

Title IX Has Done Little
for Minority Female Athletes
November 30, 2001

Welch Suggs covered athletics for the Chronicle of Higher Education *for many years, developing a familiarity and expertise with Title IX that he drew on for* A Place on the Team: The Triumph and Tragedy of Title IX *(2005). In his reporting on race, he often sought out the stories of individual athletes and leaders in the field. In this article from 2001, he surveyed both the stereotypes and the actual experiences of minority female athletes. While significant research has focused on the experience of African American women in athletics, much less attention has been given to the experiences of Hispanic, Asian, and American Indian female athletes.*

Black women don't row. Or play soccer or lacrosse. Or compete in equestrian sports. They play basketball, or they run track. Or they don't do sports at all.

That's the stereotype, and even though she breaks it herself, Brannon Johnson says there's more than a little truth to it.

"We had family basketball games growing up," Ms. Johnson, who is African-American, says of her childhood in Philadelphia. And in the neighborhood, "the height of competition was to see who could beat each other down to the corner store."

That makes Ms. Johnson, a freshman on the varsity crew at the University of Texas at Austin, the exception that proves the rule: Black women have been bypassed in the tremendous expansion of female sports under Title IX of the Education Amendments of 1972.

Nearly a third of the women shooting hoops in Division I of the

---

Welch Suggs, "Title IX Has Done Little for Minority Female Athletes—Because of Socioeconomic and Cultural Factors, and Indifference," *Chronicle of Higher Education* (November 30, 2001), 35.

140

National Collegiate Athletic Association are black, as are nearly a quarter of female track athletes.

But only 2.7 percent of the women receiving scholarships to play all other sports at predominantly white colleges in Division I are black. Yet those are precisely the sports—golf, lacrosse, and soccer, as well as rowing—that colleges have been adding to comply with Title IX, the federal law that forbids sex discrimination at institutions receiving federal funds.

All the women's sports that colleges have added over the past 14 years attract masses of white suburban girls, but very few others. Participation rates for Hispanic, Asian, and American Indian female athletes are even tinier. Even so, colleges recruit quite a few foreign women for soccer, rowing, and other sports.

Some experts blame the NCAA and the (white) women's-sports establishment for promoting sports in which minority athletes are unlikely to participate. But the problem lies deeper than that: Coaches can't be blamed for failing to recruit women of color, when so few of them show up in the clubs and tournaments that help top athletes develop. Colleges can't really be lambasted for their choices of sports, when those sports simply don't draw minority women the way track and basketball do.

Yet black women and women from other minority groups clearly are not participating in most sports as much as men and white women are. And that troubles coaches, administrators, and advocates for minority issues.

Progress . . . for Some

Title IX has been around for nearly 30 years, but only in the past 14 have colleges demonstrated measurable progress in adding opportunities for women.

Since 1987, when Congress passed a law that strengthened the enforcement of Title IX, the fastest-growing sports in the NCAA have been women's soccer, rowing, golf, and lacrosse. The numbers of teams and of athletes have doubled and in some cases tripled in all four sports.

However, the number of women's basketball and track teams has risen only about 26 percent, despite the scores of colleges that have migrated into the NCAA from the National Association of Intercollegiate Athletics over that time. (Of course, black women in basketball and track have benefited from Title IX in other ways, as colleges have spent money on those programs to improve their facilities, their coaching, and their visibility.)

College fields, courts, and rivers are now teeming with equestriennes, female soccer players, rowers, and other athletes, but almost all of them—70 percent—are white.

Women from other minority groups are similarly underrepresented in college sports: Only 1.8 percent of all female athletes are Asian, and only 3 percent are Hispanic. Coaches are happy to look further afield, though: More than 7 percent of female athletes are from other countries.

And members of all minority groups except black women have been going out for Division I sports in increased numbers since 1990–91, according to NCAA statistics. The proportions of American Indian, Asian, Hispanic, and foreign athletes on women's teams have skyrocketed, while the proportion of black women has remained steady between 13.9 and 15.6 percent over the past decade. Even so, black women continue to outnumber women of all other races except white.

A Lack of Exposure

Researchers, coaches, and athletes themselves offer a number of reasons for the dearth of black women in sports, including economics, culture, and psychology. For Tina Sloan Green, though, they all revolve around access.

Ms. Green, the director of the Black Women in Sport Foundation and a professor of physical education at Temple University, points out that most urban high schools don't have the green space needed for sports such as soccer, lacrosse, and especially golf. They don't have coaches for those sports. There is nothing to suggest to a girl that she might be successful at them.

"When you have access to a sport, either you have success, or someone else sees that they might be successful," says Ms. Green. "But the cities are so jammed up."

Ms. Green, who is African-American, has some experience in this area. As a student at Philadelphia's Girls' High School, for gifted students, she found herself with a variety of sports to play, and excelled at field hockey. At West Chester University, the lacrosse coach persuaded her to add that sport to her repertoire.

Ms. Green then coached both those sports at Temple, winning three national lacrosse titles in the 1980s with the Owls before leaving coaching in 1991 to concentrate on teaching and foundation work. Her daughter, Traci, played tennis at the University of Florida.

The Greens had access to good coaching and the junior tennis circuit, the costs of which are far out of reach for many families. Having a top-ranked junior tennis player can cost up to $30,000 a year, Ms. Green estimates. The private-club system dominates most sports like soccer and softball as well, and—unlike sports like basketball, where shoe and apparel companies cover most costs for athletes—participation is nearly as expensive as tennis.

Because virtually all of the good players go through the club system, all the coaches offering college scholarships do, too.

Access to the rich talent on the playing fields of Dallas and Houston was part of what prompted Chris Petrucelli to leave a job as coach of the University of Notre Dame's women's soccer team for the same job at Texas in 1999.

"Soccer in the U.S. is a suburban sport with a lot of little white girls running around," says Mr. Petrucelli. "There are [African-American] kids out there, but the pool we look at is very selective and relatively small. There are usually one or two minorities in it. We recruit them, but we haven't gotten them yet."

Beyond the economic hurdles, black women who do find their way into sports such as soccer or crew often have a hard time being such a small minority on their teams, according to Teresa P. Stratta, a sociologist at the University of Tennessee at Knoxville.

"There's a high correlation between the number of African-Americans on a team and their cultural expression," says Ms. Stratta, who is white. She recently conducted a two-year ethnographic study of women's teams at Temple. "A low representation of black athletes leads to more cultural inhibitions, having to put up with listening to country [music] and things like that."

If two or fewer players on a squad are black or from another minority group, they find that coaches stereotype them into certain positions, and teammates won't bond with them. It's an isolating experience, Ms. Stratta says.

"Even if you get just three or four black athletes on a team, there's a dramatic difference," she argues. "And if it gets to 30 percent to 40 percent, you have the really dynamic environment where there's an interchange, a very healthy model."

Problems at Black Colleges

Many historically black colleges and universities offer the sports that women of color shun at predominantly white institutions. But those colleges don't necessarily give students the best chances to compete.

Colleges in the Mid-Eastern and in the Southwestern Athletic Conferences—which together include all but one of the historically black colleges in Division I—tend to allocate less money for women's sports than other comparably sized predominantly white institutions in their regions. They also offer fewer playing opportunities for women, especially given that there are far more women than men at those colleges.

Most colleges in the Mid-Eastern conference, for example, average about 60-percent female, while only 40.5 percent of the athletes at those institutions are women, for a difference of nearly 20 percentage points. In the Southern Conference, which consists of colleges in roughly the same region as the Mid-Eastern league, the difference in proportions is only 12.7 points.

Colleges in the Southwestern Athletic Conference each spend an average of $607,452 on women's sports, or 29 percent of their total operating budgets for sports. Colleges in the Southland Conference, by comparison, spent just over $1-million apiece on women's sports, or 40 percent of their overall operating budgets.

Part of the reason has to do with economics: Most historically black institutions sponsor football teams, which require many male athletes and a lot of money, but don't make any profits that athletics departments could use for women's sports.

However, the same is true of many predominantly white colleges at the lower levels of Division I, yet more of them do a better job of accommodating female athletes than do most historically black colleges.

In the MEAC and the SWAC, the main concession athletics directors have made to women is adding bowling teams, which are cheap to support and don't require much training or any new facilities. The NCAA has named bowling an "emerging sport" for women, and by 1999–2000 there were 21 teams in Division I, more than any other added sport except water polo.

"Part of what we have found is that the sports at major institutions don't necessarily have strong support from our constituents at the high-school level, so there is no natural feeder system," says Charles S. Harris, commissioner of the MEAC and chairman of the NCAA's Division I Management Council.

Mr. Harris adds that the population of elementary- and high-school students is growing increasingly diverse, and that the association might face a problem if nonwhite children continue to avoid the sports that are popular right now.

No More Walk-ons

In the past, college coaches often would introduce themselves to women on campus who might make good athletes. Anita L. DeFrantz remembers walking to class at Connecticut College and seeing a long, skinny boat in front of a classroom building. "I went over to inquire, and there was a man standing there," recalls Ms. DeFrantz, who is African-American. "I didn't know he was the coach, but he said, 'This is rowing, and you'd be perfect for it.'"

"Since I'd never been perfect at anything, I thought I'd give it a go."

That encounter led her to an outstanding career in rowing, and she was named to the U.S. Olympic teams in 1976 and 1980, winning a bronze medal in the former. She is now president of the Amateur Athletic Foundation of Los Angeles and a member of the International Olympic Committee.

But her story is a little outdated, for most sports. Athletes specialize at ever-earlier ages, and college coaches recruit players with years of experience at high levels of play. The chances of someone "walking on" to a Division I soccer team today, without being recruited or having years of experience, the way Ms. DeFrantz picked up rowing in the early 1970s, are somewhere between slim and none.

Is the largely white sports establishment to blame for the lack of black women in those sports? No and yes, according to administrators and advocates.

Coaches can't be blamed for recruiting only the most skilled athletes they can find, or at least that they can get into their institutions. They're paid to win, not to provide growth opportunities for athletes who can't contribute.

Some advocates for female athletes blame the women's movement. According to Ms. Green of Temple, feminists, and particularly advocates for women's sports, have overlooked the needs of minority women.

"When you increase scholarships in these sports, you're not going to help people of color," she says. "But that's not in their line of interest. Title IX was for white women. I'm not going to say black women haven't benefited, but they have been left out."

Donna A. Lopiano, president of the Women's Sports Foundation, says Ms. Green has a point.

"The women's movement is so focused on so many gender issues that the plight of women of color, who are in double jeopardy, is oftentimes on the back burner," Ms. Lopiano, the former women's athletics director at Texas, said in an e-mail message.

Encouraging Signs

Ms. Lopiano says it has been difficult to get sports-participation statistics for college and high-school sports broken down by race, while it is relatively easy to get those numbers for the sexes. The Chronicle used the NCAA's 2001 graduation-rates statistics, which include demographic data for scholarship athletes but not for college athletes over all.

Moreover, the NCAA's rules requiring athletes to meet minimum standards for standardized-test scores to be eligible to play college sports have further restricted opportunities for black women, Ms. Green says.

Ms. Johnson is adjusting to college life and college rowing. Classes are tough, she says, but she's enjoying them as well as the rest of her two-months-and-growing adventure. She is the first in her family to attend college.

"People may look at you twice" at regattas, she says, because a black woman in a boat is still a rarity. But her teammates have made her welcome.

She got into rowing through a program for inner-city kids run by Vespers, one of the oldest rowing clubs on Philadelphia's Schuylkill River. By the time she finished high school, she was among the area's top rowers, and people along the banks of the river would yell, "Go, black girl!" as she raced by, much to her embarrassment.

Similar programs to encourage kids in urban areas to play nontraditional sports have been started by most of the national governing bodies of various sports, including the U.S. Tennis Association, the U.S. Soccer Federation, and others. They haven't borne much fruit yet, but college coaches are hoping for a parallel to the "Tiger Woods effect"—kids from unusual backgrounds getting interested in their sports, much like they did in golf when Mr. Woods emerged as a star in the late 1990s.

The NCAA and its member colleges also have encouraged these kinds of efforts through the National Youth Sports Program, a college-based effort that involves coaches and athletes in putting on clinics and organizing games for children throughout the country.

Ms. Green says that the program, which she administers at Temple, has reached children who never would have been attracted to sports before.

Eventually, black women will not have to be "firsts" anymore. But at least some of those who are firsts now are proud of it.

"I'm the first black scholarship rower at Texas," says Ms. Johnson with a smile on her face. "That makes me feel pretty good."

But she hopes that one day, they won't have to yell "Go, black girl!" at anyone in Philadelphia. Because there will be too many.

23

LUCY JANE BLEDSOE

Homophobia in Women's Sports
1997

Traditionally, one of the most potent ways to discourage women from participating in sports has been to call them "dykes," linking their desire to compete and push themselves athletically with what the dominant culture sees as deviant sexuality. Over the years, many lesbians, closeted or not, have found sports a welcome haven from heterosexual norms and an excellent place to meet like-minded women. And yet sports have never been an exclusively lesbian domain: Lesbian athletes have always been joined by legions of straight women who also felt a desire to test their own physical boundaries through competition or play. As sports have become a more acceptable outlet for girls and women, in part because of Title IX, the threat of being labeled a lesbian has lost some of its force, although homophobia—defined as an irrational fear or intolerance of gay, lesbian, bisexual, and transgendered people—is still strong in sports, causing athletes to hide or be less than open about their sexual orientation. In this piece, Lucy Jane Bledsoe, author of Sweat: Stories and a Novella, *reflects on her own experiences as a lesbian athlete in the early years of Title IX.*

Lucy Jane Bledsoe, "Team Sports Brought Us Together," *Harvard Gay and Lesbian Review*, 4, no. 3 (Spring 1997), 18–20.

On June 23rd of this year, Title IX turns 25 years old. Though the law prohibits sex discrimination of any kind in educational institutions that receive federal funding, the primary battleground for enforcement has been athletics. For those of us who came of age along with Title IX, there has been a fascinating subtext to the debate about women in sports: the shift of sports as the domain of lesbians to the domain of straight women.

Back in the early 60's, girls were not supposed to care much about sports. My second grade teacher wrote on my report card, "Lucy is too aggressive on the playground." Even then, at the age of seven, I knew that I was being called a dyke. Girls just didn't run hard, sweat, push themselves physically, or compete—at least nice girls didn't. Even so, by the time I had reached high school, I knew exactly what I wanted: to play competitive basketball with other girls who were not afraid of their own physical strength, of touching one another, of running until their muscles burned. But such an opportunity did not exist, so far as I knew nor did other girls like me.

Everything changed for me in 1973, when I was 16 and was invited to be the youth representative on a panel with Gloria Steinem in Portland, Oregon's civic auditorium. A lot happened for me that day: I learned that Gloria Steinem was an entirely different person from the press's version of her; I met my first out lesbians, who came up to congratulate me after the panel; and, most significant of all, someone handed me a copy of Public Law 92-318, which had been passed the previous year in the 92nd Congress. I have that exact same piece of paper on my desk right now, having saved it all these years. Title IX states that, "No person in the United States shall, on the basis of sex, be excluded from participation in, be denied the benefits of, or be subjected to discrimination under any education program or activity receiving Federal financial assistance." I was floored: here was a law that said I had a right to play interscholastic team sports.

I knew that my high school, like most schools in the country, was not in compliance. So, armed with my copy of Title IX and utter naivete about political action, I managed to get myself placed on the agenda of the next meeting of the Portland Public School Board. There I presented a short speech chock full of specific examples about how, in my high school, there was nothing close to equal opportunity for female athletes. There were only five options for girls who wanted to participate, and all were individual sports: golf, tennis, swimming, gymnastics, and track-and-field. Boys could also play football, basketball, baseball, and wrestling. Not only that, but the boys' teams always got use of the facilities for practice at the best times. Earlier that year I had organized a girls' basketball team, enrolled us in the city parks league, and convinced my P.E. teacher, Miss Brink (who actually looked like Ann Bannon's Beebo Brinker), to coach us. We were not an officially sanctioned team, so we had no transportation, no uniforms, no equipment, and we had to practice at six o'clock in the morning. I told the Board this and much more. Having delivered this information, I assumed that my job was done and that Portland Public schools would readily comply with Title IX.

When the minutes of that meeting came out the following week, I saw that the secretary had used the word "alleged" for each of my claims, while every one else that night "said" what they had to say. The secretary also scrambled my remarks so completely that it was hard to believe he had not done so deliberately.

A much larger brouhaha than I could have imagined blew up. There was a volley of letters to the Editor of The Oregonian. Memos flew around the city. Within a couple of days, I had twice been called a "liar" in print. The boys' basketball coach, Coach Crandall, found me in the school hall, literally pinned me to the wall, and threatened me: I would be sorry, he said, if I didn't zip up my mouth, and fast. Throughout the week, other coaches echoed his threats and the principal called me into his office to explain my claims. Didn't I understand, he asked me, that there wasn't enough money in the budget for girls' teams? That they would have to take the money out of the football and basketball budgets?

Most significant of all, however, was that I had apparently "come out." My best friend at the time was a star on the boys' basketball team. He told me that Coach Crandall had told the entire team one afternoon in the locker room that I was a dyke, and told the boys to pass the word. And he was absolutely right: I was a lesbian. Who else would risk bringing down the wrath of the entire high school male population on her head? And who else would want to create a community of girls that badly?

There were other options for all-female community at that time: women were running off to lesbian neighborhoods or forming political groups on campuses but these were not available for younger girls. Sports teams were the only place to find whole groups of girls who were, if not yet out lesbians, clearly not cheerleaders either. I played both high school and college basketball, and in all those years I can't recall one time that boys were the topic of conversation in the locker room, team buses, or practice gymnasiums. Though we didn't talk about being lesbians, our social life was a complicated web of inter-team relationships, crushes, and desire. In spite of all the lessons I had been taught about what girls should look and act like, the three stars on my high school basketball team were butch dreams-come-trues for me. Nowhere else were girls like Pam, Joan, and Cindy worshipped, but they were here—at least by me. Teams provided the crucial community structure to my coming out years. They were my lesbian training ground.

Besides providing an alternative community—alternative, that is, to other social gatherings for girls that age—sports provided me with a powerful source of knowledge about my body, an opportunity that was just as rare as a community of strong girls. It is now fashionable to portray feminism as a viewpoint, even a glorification, of victimhood. This cry of "victim politics" is particularly loud when women talk about assaults on our bodies, including rape, battery, incest, and mandatory appearance standards. Of course, the name-calling is intended to shut feminists up and to distort the full picture for the culture at large, which it has to some degree. But feminism is about choosing alternatives. And sports are the perfect paradigm for this stand against victimization: for choosing a positive relationship to our female bodies. Sports have been a big part of so many lesbians' lives because they provide the opportunity to find and express strength, skill, precision, and sheer physical joy. Athletics teach women to become comfortable in their bodies and to overcome physical fear, lessons that were hard to find anywhere else in the 60's and 70's. We—the girls with whom I played ball—felt like anything but victims. We were flying in the face of the people we were supposed to be—and that made us feel like we were flying, period.

A lot has changed since my youth. In the 25 years since the passage of Title IX, compliance has moved at a snail's pace, but it has moved. In 1972 only one in 27 girls played high school sports. The number is now one in three. Women make up 37 percent of collegiate athletes, up 22 percent since 1992. There are now two pro women's basketball leagues, and both high school and college women's sports have become much more competitive.

However, in the fight to gain equality in women's sports, lesbians have paid a huge price. As more and more straight women claim their right to play, homophobia has become increasingly prevalent on the courts and fields, and in the locker rooms. Women's sports promoters are working hard to clean the dyke image off the face of women's athletics. At a recent professional women's basketball game, the announcer must have told the audience 25 times (one time for each year of Title IX's existence) that this was a family event. One young man, that same evening, proposed marriage to his girlfriend—on mike in front of the whole basketball audience. This was arranged in advance by the basketball promoters, who were clearly thrilled to present this most sanctioned expression of heterosexuality to the crowd. Many college coaches strongly encourage their female athletes to adopt very feminine behavior, and they provide strict dress and hair codes, all to separate the terms "female athlete" and "dyke." And this hurts. In the 60's and 70's, teams were our domain. No woman would have a place on the team today if it weren't for the lesbians—and straight women who were not afraid to be called lesbians—who fought long and hard for that place.

Some lesbians are fighting back—Martina [Navratilova], of course, for one—and only time will tell if team sports remain an important source of community and self-esteem for young lesbians. But at least one study leads one to conclude that they will not. On March 28, 1997, Donna Shalala, Secretary of Health and Human Services, announced the publication of the first-ever Health and Human Services report on girls and sports. One finding of the report was that homophobia limits the potential of some girls to derive positive experiences from sports. Wouldn't it be ironic if, by complying with Title IX, schools ruined sports for young lesbians? It is a sad possibility that the mainstreaming of yet another subculture—the world of lesbian jocks—may mean excluding the original members of that subculture. Should I feel lucky that I had to work so hard for a place on the team? I do know that fighting that fight, as well as being a young lesbian athlete, taught me lessons that guide me still today.

Title IX is celebrating its silver anniversary and my own Title IX story has a bright silver lining. By my senior year in high school, Portland was in compliance and we would have a basketball program for girls. There was only one problem: No one would coach us. At that time, I was the editor of the school literary magazine and mainly hung out with the artsy crowd who didn't understand my jock side. We all made fun of the coaches, particularly Stan Stanton, the head football and wrestling coach. He looked the part perfectly with his big beer pot and ruddy face, a dedicated "old boy." Or so it seemed. The previous year, when I was being called names in the boys' locker room and being threatened by the other male coaches at the school, Coach

Stanton approached me in the hall one morning. I held my books in front of me like a shield, figuring I was going to get it again. I had known Stanton for years since both of my older brothers had been first-string quarterbacks for him, but I didn't expect any mercy. I tried to avoid eye contact and kept walking fast. To my surprise, Coach Stanton threw an arm around my shoulders and walked the length of the hallway with me—an amazingly public show of support for me and against his colleagues. "I'm with you all the way, kiddo," he said and hugged me. So much for stereotypes.

At the last minute, when it looked like the girls' basketball team would play without a coach, Coach Stanton gave up boys' wrestling to coach us. And coach us he did. We won and won and won, taking the City title and going all the way to the finals for the State Championship.

On the Saturday before that game, Coach Crandall—the boys' coach who had called me a dyke in the locker room—pulled rank. He was officially the head coach of the entire basketball program, or so he claimed, which meant he could take over coaching us for the State Championship game. He called a couple of special practices and taught us a whole new defense. The night of the big game, he sat in the head coach's chair. I will never forget the look of disgust and defeat on the face of Coach Stanton, who sacrificed so much to lead us to the finals, sitting in the assistant coach's chair.

At half-time we trailed by 17 points. Coach Stanton risked his job by standing up and telling his boss to sit down and be quiet. He called us into a huddle, told us to return to the defense he had taught us, and we overcame our opponent's huge lead to win the Championship.

24

NATIONAL COALITION FOR WOMEN AND GIRLS IN EDUCATION

Title IX at 30: Report Card on Gender Equity
2002

In June 2002, the thirtieth anniversary of Title IX's passage, the National Coalition for Women and Girls in Education issued a report card on gender equity. While mindful of the progress that had been made, the report highlighted how much more needed to be done to achieve gender equity in education. The report surveyed major areas affected by Title IX and then issued a letter grade for each: for example, math and science, B–; sexual harassment, C; technology, D+; employment, C–; and treatment of pregnant and parenting students, C+. How did athletics fare? C+.

Athletics: C+

For many people, Title IX is synonymous with expanded opportunities in athletics. Women's and girls' increased participation in sports, the impressive achievements of the nation's female athletes, their stunning advances in summer and winter Olympic Games, and the creation of nationally televised professional women's basketball and soccer leagues demonstrate Title IX's success. It takes a large and vibrant base of general sports participants and 15 to 20 years of elite athlete support to create an Olympic gold medalist or professional athlete—years in which an athlete is given access to quality coaching, sports facilities, weight rooms, athletic scholarships, and competition. Before Title IX, women and girls were precluded from taking advantage of most athletic opportunities in school, but the outcome of equal opportunity on the playing fields is becoming more apparent.

Still, Olympic medals and professional sports contracts are not what Title IX is all about. Rather, the quest for equal opportunity in sports

National Coalition for Women and Girls in Education, *Title IX at 30: Report Card on Gender Equity* (Washington, D.C.: National Coalition for Women and Girls in Education, 2002), 14–18, 20.

has always been about the physiological, sociological, and psychological benefits of sports and physical activity participation. Research studies commissioned by the Women's Sports Foundation in 1998 and 2000 found that girls who play sports enjoy greater physical and emotional health and are less likely to engage in a host of risky health behaviors (i.e., drug use, smoking, and drinking) than nonparticipants. Other studies have linked sports participation to reduced incidences of breast cancer and osteoporosis later in life. Yet compared to boys, girls enjoy 30 percent fewer opportunities to participate in high school and college sports and are twice as likely to be inactive. Much distance remains between the current status of women and girls in sports and the ultimate goal of gender equity.

PARTICIPATION RATES AND RESOURCE ALLOCATION

Prior to 1972, women and girls looking for opportunities for athletic competition were more likely to try out for cheerleading or secure places in the bleachers as spectators. In 1971 fewer than 295,000 girls participated in high school varsity athletics, accounting for just 7 percent of all high school varsity athletes. The outlook for college women was equally grim: Fewer than 30,000 females competed in intercollegiate athletics. Low participation rates reflected the lack of institutional commitment to providing athletics programming for women. Before Title IX, female college athletes received only 2 percent of overall athletic budgets, and athletic scholarships for women were virtually nonexistent.

Title IX has changed the playing field significantly. By 2001 nearly 2.8 million girls participated in athletics, representing 41.5 percent of varsity athletes in U.S. high schools—an increase of more than 847 percent from 1971. Progress on college campuses also has been impressive. Today 150,916 women compete in intercollegiate sports, accounting for 43 percent of college varsity athletes—an increase of more than 403 percent from 1971. Contrary to media reports, men's participation levels at both the high school and college level have also increased.

While significant, these gains still stop short of providing girls and women with their fair share of opportunities to compete. In 1999–2000 female students represented about 54 percent of the student body at four-year colleges, yet only 23 percent of all NCAA Division I colleges provided women with athletic opportunities within five percentage points of female student enrollment. This percentage increased from 9 percent in 1995–96.

Although the resources and benefits allocated to female athletes also have improved significantly since Title IX's passage, they also fall far short of what equity requires. After 30 years, the gap is still significant and closing much too slowly. Institutions are not exercising restraint on men's sports expenditures while women's sports catch up.

— In the past four years, for every new dollar going into athletics at the Division I and Division II levels, male sports received 58 cents while female sports received 42 cents.

— Each year male athletes receive $133 million or 36 percent more than female athletes in college athletic scholarships at NCAA member institutions.

— In Division I, colleges spent an average of $2,983 per female athlete compared to $3,786 for male athletes.

No national data on expenditures exist for girls' and boys' interscholastic sports, but anecdotal evidence suggests that similar financial disparities also exist at the elementary and secondary levels.

COACHES, ADMINISTRATORS, AND OTHER ATHLETIC PERSONNEL

Women in coaching, athletic administration, and other sports positions lack the improved opportunities enjoyed by female students and athletes since Title IX's enactment. In the early 1970s women head coaches led 90 percent of women's collegiate teams. By the 2001–02 school year, female head coaches led only 44 percent of women's intercollegiate athletic teams, the lowest total since the passage of Title IX. This number is down from 47.7 percent in 1995–96. Since 2000, 90 percent of the available head coaching positions in women's athletics have gone to men. A similar decline in the percentage of women coaching girls' teams can be witnessed at the high school level.

To make matters worse, the loss of coaching opportunities in women's sports has not been offset by a corresponding increase in opportunities for women to coach men's teams. To the contrary, women are virtually shut out of these jobs, holding only 2 percent of the coaching positions in men's collegiate sports, a percentage that has remained constant over the last 30 years. No signs indicate a slowing in the downward trend.

Women's college basketball, considered by most to be the greatest economic success among all women's collegiate sports, is one of few exceptions to diminishing coaching opportunities for women. The number of women intercollegiate basketball coaches has remained relatively constant over the past 10 years, with women currently holding 62.8 percent of these head coaching jobs. Among 24 women's NCAA championship sports, however, female coaches rank in the majority in only seven.

The impact of such sex discrimination on coaching opportunities for women is exacerbated by the striking disparity in the salaries paid to coaches of men's and women's teams. At the Division I level, men's basketball head coaches average $149,700. By contrast, women's basketball head coaches average just $91,300: 61 cents to every dollar paid to men. This trend continues at the assistant coach level, where men's basketball assistant coaches average $44,000 while women's basketball assistant coaches average $34,000. Only in fencing, volleyball, and tennis, the sports paying the lowest salaries to coaches of male teams, do coaches of women's sports receive equal or greater pay than coaches of the equivalent male sports.

Athletic directors at the college level are also predominately male (83.1 percent). As the status and salary of these positions increase, female representation decreases (8.4 percent in Division I versus 25.5 percent in Division III). Males also dominate the positions of sports information director (87.7 percent) and athletic trainer (72.2 percent). As the competitiveness of a division and average salary increases, women's representation in these athletics positions also decreases. This trend remains true for every position except for head coaching jobs, for which gender representation in Division I and Division III is equal, although average salaries are not. . . .

Given the absence of equal opportunity after 30 years, OCR [Office for Civil Rights] is not providing adequate leadership in enforcement efforts. In 2001 OCR initiated only two Title IX athletics reviews of institutions. Since Title IX's inception, not one institution has had its federal funding withdrawn because it is in violation of Title IX. OCR's lack of enforcement coupled with an increase in Title IX lawsuits suggests aggrieved parties are required to seek relief through the court system. Parties filing lawsuits incur considerable costs and risk retribution. In light of the numbers of schools still not in compliance, OCR needs to step up its enforcement activities.

RECOMMENDATIONS

—Congress should mandate data collection on the participation of high school students in physical education and high school athletics programs as part of the administration's proposal for the reauthorization of the Office for Educational Research and Improvement.

—The Department of Education should support the continuation of existing strong compliance standards and increase OCR enforcement of these standards.

—To encourage the filing of actionable complaints, OCR should develop a standard complaint form with a checklist of alleged Title IX violations.

—School athletic administrations should use the Equal Employment Opportunity Commission guidelines (www.eeoc.gov/regs/index.html) to make sure coaches of male and female sports receive equal treatment.

25

SECRETARY'S COMMISSION ON OPPORTUNITY IN ATHLETICS

Open to All: Title IX at Thirty

2003

In 2002, Secretary of Education Roderick Paige created the Commission on Opportunity in Athletics, a fifteen-member federal advisory panel charged with looking once again at the issues and debates surrounding Title IX and its implementation. Given President George W. Bush's conservative political agenda, many Title IX supporters feared that the commission was the first step in an attempt to weaken the law, but the panel's final report, issued on February 26, 2003, did not recommend major changes in the law's enforcement. The report opened with a section called "The Spectrum of Opinions," a sampling of testimony presented to the committee in the course of its hearings. These voices provide a compact summary of many of the controversies and challenges still surrounding Title IX three decades after its passage.

"The word quota does not appear . . . What we were really looking for was equal opportunity for young women and for girls in the educa-

U.S. Department of Education, Secretary's Commission on Opportunity in Athletics, *Open to All: Title IX at Thirty* (Washington, D.C.: U.S. Department of Education, 2003), 7–12.

tional system of the United States of America. Equality of opportunity. Equality. That shouldn't really be a controversial subject in a nation that now for 200 years has prided itself in equal justice." — Birch Bayh, Former United States Senator

"We just want to make a good thing better. We want something to help all Americans." — Rod Paige, United States Secretary of Education

"If the decision is made to eliminate sports for gender-equity reasons, it is because institutions have chosen this path rather than pursuing other options, not because Title IX dictates such action." — Judith Sweet, vice-president for championships and senior woman administrator, National Collegiate Athletic Association

"It is really the schools that are setting out those arbitrary limits, and what Title IX is saying in participation terms is how do we decide whether or not those schools' limits are fair and equitable?" — Marcia Greenberger, co-president, National Women's Law Center

"The unfortunate truth is that Title IX has evolved into something never intended. The act was intended to expand opportunity. The interpretation by the Office for Civil Rights and the evolved enforcement has turned into a quota program. Title IX is a good law with bad interpretation." — Carol Zaleski, former president and executive director, USA Swimming

"It is good, fair legislation, and most importantly, it should be enforced. Title IX does not drop men's sports programs. Title IX is about equal opportunities." — Peggy Bradley-Doppes, athletics director, University of North Carolina-Wilmington

"Like others before, I support Title IX as it is written. I do not, however, support some of the applications and interpretations that have evolved over the years, and I see nothing wrong with examining all aspects of Title IX in its 30th anniversary year." — Charles "Rick" Taylor, athletics director, Northwestern University

"The three-part test (for Title IX compliance) is flexible, lawful, and reflects fundamental principles of equality." — Athena Yiamouyiannis, executive director, National Association for Girls and Women in Sports

"I came 1,000 miles just to ask for 21st century reform to one of the most powerful pieces of legislation for women that we've seen. Let our sons play." — Beverly Brandon, parent, Forth Worth, TX

"As it stands, the law eliminates the actual interest and ability of students as a factor in the design of varsity programs. Institutions are responsible for the raw universe of people, not the universe of students who have the varsity ability and interest, but the universe of all students, whether or not they care to be involved in varsity athletics. . . . Universities must have full discretion and responsibility to determine the breadth and scope of their athletic offerings just as they do for their academic programs." —Beverly Ledbetter, general counsel, Brown University

"I am here to take you on a short ride in Thelma and Louise's car if you think it's fair and just to limit a girl's opportunity to play sports based on her response to an interest survey." —Geena Davis, actress and amateur archer

"I will never complain about women getting more opportunities. I will complain about Marquette University cutting their wrestling team—that didn't cost them one penny because it was funded by outside sources—simply so it would not fall afoul of the proportionality standard; simply so they wouldn't get dragged into court and lose." —Leo Kocher, head wrestling coach, University of Chicago

"Between 1993 and 1999 alone 53 men's golf teams, 39 men's track teams, 43 wrestling teams, and 16 baseball teams have been eliminated. The University of Miami's diving team, which has produced 15 Olympic athletes, is gone." —Christine Stolba, fellow, Independent Women's Forum

"It is not Title IX that is the issue, it is the interpretation. The interpretation has in many ways been illogical, unfair and contrary to Congressional intent." —Grant Teaff, executive director, American Football Coaches Association

"And I can tell you from personal experience that women who play sports in college, any sport, are significantly enhancing their chances of maximizing professional opportunities." —Val Ackerman, president, Women's National Basketball Association

"The proportionality test purports to be a test of gender fairness, but its logic rests on one critical and dubious assumption, that males and females at every college in the nation have an equal desire to play competitive team sports." —Katherine Kersten, senior fellow, Center of the American Experiment

"I say to the Commission that Title IX is not broken and should not be tweaked or watered down. What is broken, however, is the college football experience and the outrageous expenditures that are made in an attempt to win the 'arms race.' . . . The excesses in every area of the game from roster sizes to the size of coaching staff to the outlandish travel arrangements and the piano players for the recruits, could all be combined to pay for several minor sports programs." —Barbara Schroeder, director of athletics, Regis University

"I have worked closely with the Office for Civil Rights staff on many issues and for many years. You have a dedicated and overworked group of folks there, but often I sense they are restrained in their exercise of common sense by being forced to count shower heads and to do everything on the basis of numbers, by the enforcement regulations rather than the law itself, and occasionally by someone feeling that he or she knows more about higher education administration than does the entire university hierarchy." —George Shur, general counsel, Northern Illinois University

"I am attempting to lead that effort to bring our football program back because you cannot underestimate the importance football has on a black college campus. It enhances enrollment, alumni giving, and the marching bands." —Teresa Check, athletic director, Central State University

"If the current trend of program elimination continues, we will suffer the consequences, as will be evidenced by the absence of American athletes on the medals' podium at future Olympic games." —Marty Mankamyer, president, United States Olympics Committee

"Administrators are fearful that test three means that if two women—this is what you hear all the time in my world—if two women show up and want to start a team, then the interest is there and the women must be accommodated, so how do I decide whether they're really supposed to start a team or not?" —Debbie Corum, associate commissioner, Southeastern Conference

"If I were to use the Florida Community College System as an example, the average age of students attending is 31. . . . I would not mean to imply that men and women at this age do not have athletic interests, but their ability to take advantage of opportunities is definitely different." —Karen Sykes, president, National Junior College Athletic Association

"I was here in 1972 when there was really no interest on the part of girls to participate, and the high school participation at that time was eight percent. The schools were forced to offer opportunity, and my goodness, it's now up to 42 percent." —Christine Grant, associate professor and former athletic director, University of Iowa

"We found that 75 percent of our (school) districts were not significantly in compliance with Title IX based on questions about their written policies, their designating a Title IX coordinator, their informing students and parents about their grievance procedures and their rights." —Susan Hinrichsen, assistant executive director, Illinois High School Association

"Our accountability is based on local control and public involvement. . . . As a superintendent and a principal and working with local boards, we believe we want the state and feds to stay out of our business most of the time." —Griff Powell, retired Illinois high school superintendent

"Do you remember when 'girl sports' was an oxymoron? Do you remember when being involved in high school athletics for girls meant acting as timekeeper at the boys swimming meet? Or being a cheerleader?" —Linda Hertz, parent, Colorado Springs, CO

"From the purely numerical standpoint, the high school is overwhelmingly where the Title IX action is. Although the collegiate level disputes have attracted more public notice, we have 20 times the number of participants in our nation's high schools." —Robert Gardner, chief operating officer, National Federation of High School Associations

"The judicial interpretations have clearly transformed the statute from a nondiscrimination statute into an equal opportunity statute." —Col. Billy Walker, associate director of athletics and head of the Department of Physical Education, U.S. Air Force Academy

"Only 5 percent participate in intercollegiate athletics. Ninety-five percent of the students are spectators. . . ." —Brian Snow, general counsel, Colorado State University

"On a per school basis the number of male athletes has decreased by 7.7 percent between 1981 and 2000. The number of female athletes has increased over that timeframe by 52.6 percent." —Corey Bray, assistant director of research, Education Services, NCAA

"Between 1985 and 2001 male athletes have lost 57,700 athletes. . . . In addition, women athletes have gained a real rate of 51,967 athletes over the course of this period of time. That's a rate of gain of 2,735 women athletes per year." —Jerome Kravitz, consultant to the U.S. Department of Education and professor at Howard University

"It's OK to have sympathy for that walk-on. It's OK to have sympathy for every male who loses his opportunity to play, but you must have unbiased sympathy. You have to feel just as sorry for every woman who didn't have the chance to play, for women who still, at the institutional level, are not getting chances to play, who are not getting benefits, and you simply can't discriminate on the basis of sex in your empathy." —Donna Lopiano, executive director, Women's Sports Foundation

"Twenty-three years ago, seven years after the statute was passed, the policy interpretation was written by government bureaucrats with the input of some outside groups under a political deadline under a political hook." —Kimberly Schuld, former director, Play Fair

"To us Title IX is not social activism that favors the minority. To us, it's a law designed to ensure that fully one-half of the American population gets basic rights in the classroom and on the playing field." —Rosa Perez, president, Canada College

26

SUSAN CAMPBELL

Cheers for Title IX

June 22, 2005

As the thirty-third anniversary of Title IX approached, the Hartford Courant *asked readers to write in about what Title IX had meant to them. The newspaper received over seventy replies, of which the following were published on June 22, 2005. Starting with the mother of University of Connecticut basketball star Rebecca Lobo, the writers give a more per-*

Susan Campbell, "Cheers for Title IX," *Hartford Courant* (June 22, 2005), D1.

sonal slant on the law than that of the ongoing debates in Washington. There really is no turning back.

While she was growing up, I repeatedly told her what my mother had told me: You can be whatever you want. It wasn't until she looked at me and said she wanted to play football for the NFL that I began to question the wisdom of my words. When she wrote to Red Auerbach, the general manager of the Boston Celtics, to proclaim that she would one day play for his team, I was confronted with the reality and its accompanying sadness that she could not be whatever she wanted.

I had not yet heard of Title IX.

Thanks to the efforts of many women who refused to quit and who stood up for their daughters and mine, the door to opportunity was opened in 1972 for both boys and girls to escape gender stereotypes and to explore areas of interest not available in the past. For my daughter, the path ultimately led to participation in intercollegiate sports, where she benefited from the commitment to gender equity of those who came before her. She was able to fulfill the dream of becoming a professional athlete. More importantly, she has joined the ranks of so many others who have demonstrated you can be whatever you want, regardless of gender, when opportunity is present. Thank you, Title IX.

—RuthAnn Lobo, Simsbury

Growing up outside Madison, Wis., I always had a league to play in. I was able to run free around the bases in tee-ball and play all through my childhood.

Title IX allowed me a chance to play, but most importantly Title IX allowed me to become an obsessed, passionate, die-hard sports fan. Title IX made it acceptable for girls to play sports, but also to watch. Soon, I was enamored with watching all types of sports on television at all times. I even dislocated my shoulder during the Badger/Purdue football game last season. My body went one way, and my shoulder went another when Scott Starks recovered the fumble for a touch-down. I put my shoulder back in, an ice pack on and toughed it out for the rest of the Badgers' amazing come-from-behind win. I feel it was worth it, after all, because Starks' fumble recovery was voted ESPN and Pontiac's play of the year in college football.

I am 19, but I understand the importance of Title IX. My dream to become a sportscaster is possible because of that fateful day back in

June of 1972. I cannot imagine a better fit in my life. I have the knowledge, the work ethic, but most of all I have the passion. Title IX
allowed me that passion.

—Emily Kumlien, Verona, WI

Both men and women agree that Title IX's impact on collegiate sports
brought a flood of change. That flood brought much-needed relief for
thousands of student athletes, or washed away the dreams of thousands of athletes, depending on your perspective . . . and gender.

Like the Civil Rights legislation that preceded it, this law's intention
was to make opportunities available to a group of people to whom
these opportunities were previously closed. Indeed, as the law was
written, that was the intent, and undoubtedly it accomplished great
things for girls and young women. Today, it is difficult to imagine a
time when girls were relegated to the sidelines as cheerleaders only.
My daughter benefited from this and had opportunities that were not
there for her mother. As a parent and as a girls' team coach, I'm aware
of the positive impact sports have upon the lives of girls.

But this legislation, by the way it has been enforced and the way
that enforcement has been defended and politicized, has resulted
in considerable collateral damage for young male athletes. This is
Title IX's dirty little secret. Although not in the original legislation, the
law has been enforced through the use of a rigid quota system. This
system has resulted in the loss of over 400 men's programs since
1972. Programs hit particularly hard include track, baseball, swimming and wrestling, which lost 134 programs. Men's gymnastics has
all but disappeared. The team I wrestled on in college, Central Connecticut, axed its program shortly after I was graduated. My college
experience would have been far different and far emptier if I had gone
to college a few years later.

We should not be choosing between our sons and daughters. We
need to return to the spirit of Title IX, for all of our children.

—Joe Miragliuolo, Pomfret Center

In the early '60s, I pedaled my blue Schwinn bike to all my little
brother's Little League games behind the Town Hall in Somers. I
stood behind the back-stop fence with my brother's old glove on and
waited and waited to be asked to play. It never happened, but I didn't
give up my dream of some day being able to play league sports. The
best I could do was practice my skills one-on-one with my brother.
Occasionally, the neighborhood boys would grudgingly let me play if
they needed more outfielders but would often skip my turn at bat.

Being the tallest girl at Hartford Public High School in the late '60s, I was the center for their women's basketball team. Back then, coaching was nonexistent, and our "season" consisted of four games total against Bulkeley and Weaver, if all five of us were available. No one came to watch us play, but I was finally playing a league sport, although today it would be considered a pathetic imitation.

Timing was such that I wasn't able to reap the benefits of Title IX, but I was ecstatic when it became law. It meant no more little girls' having to wait on the sidelines aching to play. Every time I see or read about a woman at the top of her game, I say a silent "thank you."

—Elin O'Leary Walpole, Glastonbury

Because of Title IX, my 12-year-old daughter is on a multitude of sports teams. She plays basketball, soccer and swims. She plays on girls' team in organized leagues, and in school plays on co-ed teams. She can play for the love of these games, with little of the prejudices that existed only a few decades ago.

Title IX helped level the playing field. While it is important in its passage, one must not forget all of those girls and women (who are now our mothers, grandmothers and aunts) that played sports prior to the passage of Title IX and helped set the course for it to happen in the first place.

—John Molina, Rocky Hill

Beside her name and portrait in the yearbook, it says French Club and Future Teachers of America. Although she enjoys sports recreationally—like swimming and tennis—she has never been a member of any sports team. It is 1970.

Thirty-four years later in a different yearbook, the portrait of a girl with the same chestnut curls and sunny smile has similar activities, including French Club, Yearbook and Newspaper, but also Swimming, Volleyball, Softball and even Stickball. The 1970 high school graduate is now grown and has a daughter. This is her. This is me.

Title IX created something for me that my mother never had, the opportunity to participate in any sport that piques my interest. I have never been afraid of any stigma that may be attached to girls' playing sports, or taunting from people who believe that my sports should be for "boys only." I've been able to enjoy myself while learning the value of strength, drive and teamwork. Over the years of being in sports teams, I have shown my true colors not only to my teammates but also myself—and in return teammates, coaches and spectators have helped me to recognize when to shoot, when to pass, when to cheer, and that there is never an excuse to quit. I've been taught that, although boys and girls may have different physical abilities, neither is more or less deserving of participation. And although we may not always win, I am not intimidated when my softball team scrimmages against the boys' baseball team. I know that I belong on that field as much as the boys do.

—Maureen Rousseau, Farmington

I was a typical little girl in 1979 with a frilly dress and shiny Mary Janes. My mother placed me in ballet and figure skating, two activities any little girl would have loved to do. The minute we would arrive back home, I would strip off the lace and throw on my favorite shirt. It was a blue football jersey with the number 12 on it. I thought it was so cool when I wore it. I put on my blue helmet and rode my skateboard to my friend's house, never once thinking about ballet or figure skating.

One day in figure class, I sprinted across the ice and skidded on my blades, throwing a wave of ice spray. My coach called me over and exclaimed, "That was not ladylike!"

I skated away from him and to my mom watching in horror from the bleachers. "I want to play hockey, Mom," I proclaimed. The next thing I knew, that blue helmet became my hockey helmet, with the addition of $100 worth of equipment from the swap shop.

I was one of three girls in the Enfield Mites program. Title IX allowed me to mature in a non-gender-specific environment. I played on co-ed teams through college.

Currently, I am on another team I never thought I could play on. I am a firefighter. Without the opportunity my mom allowed me in 1979, I would still be wearing lace and Mary Janes. I probably would still have a jersey hidden in the closet.

—Melissa Roming, Rocky Hill

I walked into the classroom in 1974, a freshman entering the rarefied air of the economics department. Everyone sat at the large conference table worn with ruts created by years of note-taking by privileged young men. Who was I—daughter of a mason, granddaughter of a seam-stress, name ending in a vowel—to presume I could hold my own?

My professor made it abundantly clear that I was the unwelcome interloper in this classroom filled with [Y] chromosomes. He sent me to the blackboard each and every class. His blatantly discriminatory treatment of me would lead to my lifetime passion for women's rights.

At the end of it, I learned two things: a hell of a lot of economics, and that sitting at that table was not easy but necessary.

So what does this have to do with Title IX?

Title IX has helped us to get to where we are on today's campuses—to a place that, while improving, is still not great. Its provisions have opened up opportunities for my daughters, opportunities to play soccer and basketball the way they were meant to be played, full court, with no limit on the number of passes. It has allowed my baby girl, a beautiful 17-year-old high school student, smart and creative and funny, to work toward becoming an architect. I don't pretend that Title IX provisions have led to a rosy future for all girls and boys, but I certainly am grateful that my daughters can take a seat at the table at which I was not welcome.

—Lucy L. Brakoniecki, Glastonbury

My parents gave me a red leather baseball glove when I was 8 years old. I oiled it, tied an old tie around it with a ball inside, and put it under my mattress. I wanted to play Little League just like my brother. He was a pitcher, had a cool uniform and played in a ballpark with a scoreboard and bleachers.

He practiced with me in the backyard. I put a sponge in my glove because he threw so hard, my hand would turn red and swollen.

I could catch, but I couldn't play.

I wanted to play sports, but the only sports offered to girls was softball and Pop Warner cheerleading.

Just before I entered high school, Title IX was passed. I was on the first volleyball team in my high school and became an all-conference player. I learned how to rebound and fight for a ball under the basket for the basketball team. My mom was the only person to come to the afternoon games. When I finally beat my nemesis in the MBIAC tennis league, my family spray-painted huge congratulations on a big sheet and hung it in front of the house.

I became part of a team, a family, when I joined the college tennis team as a freshman. Being a team player has changed me as a person. The need to be flexible and work with others for a common goal is essential; that is a skill that I want to teach to my children.

I wanted my daughters to experience the high of working together, the satisfaction of a job well done. The first time I saw my daughters play basketball, I found myself on the sidelines, sitting in a folding chair, with tears in my eyes—they could play!

—Kathy Waddington, Granby

Age: 11

Sport: Baseball (not softball).

Field position: Second base or catcher, with a slight favoritism toward second base.

Hometown team: Dodgers.

Favorite professional team: Don't be silly. The Red Sox.

Favorite school subject: Writing.

Goal: To play next to Jason Varitek in Boston.

—Michaela Roche, Bristol

The girls ruled on Lynmoor Street in Milford during the late 1960s to mid-1970s. There were pick-up basketball games, Wiffle ball, tennis, Milford Recreation softball, elementary school flag football, plus track and field.

We ruled.

We had no appreciation for how lucky we were. There were parents and teachers who pitched, coached, drove and cheered us along. We were also very good athletes.

For those entering freshman year of high school in the fall of 1972, there were no organized sports for girls in Connecticut. Instead, we took the bus home after school and did nothing. A new high school was opening in town during the fall of 1973, a palatial facility with one of the nicest gymnasiums in the state. The thought of boys only playing on this floor was unnerving, so we learned about political activism.

Before the school opened and as the new administrators were named, the girls contacted these people and members of the Board of Education. We organized our thoughts, composed letters, attended public meetings and pitched our case for funding of girls sports on the high school level. Concurrently, Title IX, a law banning discrimination in any educational program that receives federal funding, went into effect. Whether prompted by law or not, local officials funded girls high school sports beginning that fall.

The girls from Lynmoor Street would play on that new gymnasium floor with the high-intensity mercury-vapor lights and crisp sound system. We would go on to win a state championship in volleyball, produce all-state performers and participate in Division I college athletics. With opportunity, high achievement followed. There is no turning back.

—M. M. Winfield, Milford

A Chronology of Title IX
and Related Events
(1964–2014)

1964 Title VII of the Civil Rights Act of 1964 prohibits discrimination in employment based on race, sex, national origin, or religion

1966 Commission on Intercollegiate Athletics for Women (CIAW) formed

National Organization for Women (NOW) founded

1970,
1971 Representative Edith Green holds hearings on sex discrimination in higher education

1971 Association for Intercollegiate Athletics for Women (AIAW) founded

1972 Equal Rights Amendment passes Congress

Title IX signed into law by President Richard Nixon

1973 Billie Jean King beats Bobby Riggs in "The Battle of the Sexes"

1974 Javits Amendment saying that Title IX regulations must take into account the nature of particular sports passed

Women's Sports Foundation established

1975 Department of Health, Education, and Welfare issues final guidelines for enforcing Title IX

Tower Amendment to exempt revenue-producing sports from Title IX coverage dies in committee

1978 Mandatory compliance date for all high schools and postsecondary institutions

Women's Professional Basketball League (WBL) begins play

1979 HEW issues Policy Interpretation on Title IX compliance (the three-prong test) regarding athletics

Cannon v. University of Chicago allows a private party to bring suit to enforce Title IX without first exhausting all administrative remedies

Department of Education established; Office for Civil Rights continues as main oversight agency for Title IX

1982 AIAW dissolves and NCAA takes control of women's intercollegiate athletics

Women's Professional Basketball League folds

1984 *Grove City College v. Bell* holds that Title IX applies only to programs receiving direct federal funding

Joan Benoit wins first women's marathon at 1984 Olympic games in Los Angeles

1988 Civil Rights Restoration Act (passed over President Reagan's veto) restores institution-wide scope of Title IX

1990 Office for Civil Rights publishes Investigator's Manual to help institutions evaluate whether they are in compliance with Title IX

1991 NCAA undertakes its first comprehensive survey of the status of women athletes in its member institutions

1992 *Franklin v. Gwinnett County Public Schools* allows monetary damages in Title IX lawsuits

1993 *Favia v. Indiana University of Pennsylvania* rules that monetary and budgetary difficulties are not an excuse for not complying with Title IX

Gonyo v. Drake University rules that men may not use Title IX to claim sex discrimination when men's teams are cut

1994 Equity in Athletics Disclosure Act requires colleges and universities to collect and publicize annual information on athletic participation by sex

1995 House Subcommittee on Postsecondary Education holds hearings on 3-prong test for participation and compliance

Cohen et al. v. Brown University affirms the Office for Civil Rights' three-prong test

1996 Clarification letter on Title IX compliance issued by the Office for Civil Rights on three-prong test

U.S. women take gold medal in soccer at 1996 Olympic games in Atlanta

Debut of American Basketball League (ABL)

1997 NBA-sponsored Women's National Basketball Association starts up

1998   U.S. beats Canada for first women's ice hockey gold medal at 1998 Olympics in Nagano, Japan

American Basketball League files for bankruptcy

1999   U.S. soccer team beats China 5–4 before 90,000 spectators (a record for a women's sporting event) at the Rose Bowl to win Women's World Cup

2002   National Wrestling Coaches Association files suit against the Department of Education

2003   Secretary's Commission on Opportunity in Athletics issues *Open to All: Title IX at 30*

Further clarification letter reaffirms Title IX guidelines and jurisdiction

National Wrestling Coaches Association suit dismissed

2005   Department of Education allows colleges to use email to survey student interest

2005   Tennessee's Pat Summit becomes the winningest basketball coach, male or female, in NCAA history

2008   Women make up 42% of competitors at the Summer Olympics in Beijing

2009   Danika Patrick finishes third in the Indianapolis 500

2010   Department of Education rescinds email option to survey student interest

University of Connecticut women's basketball team wins 90 consecutive games, including two national championships

2013   Fortieth anniversary of Billie Jean King-Bobby Riggs "Battle of the Sexes"

2014   Women's ski jumping debuts at Winter Olympics in Sochi, Russia

Questions for Consideration

1. What is gender equity? What do words like *comparable* and *equal* mean in the context of athletics? Is the goal equality of opportunity, or equality of results?

2. What was the relationship between the revival of feminism in the 1970s and the passage of Title IX? Have issues of women's sports been an important item on the feminist agenda since? If not, why?

3. Has the impact of Title IX been exaggerated by ascribing all changes in women's sports to it? How many of these changes would have happened without the law?

4. What has been lost and what has been gained as women's sports increasingly mirror men's?

5. Is athletic reform possible, or are the popular forces driving competition and commercialization too strong?

6. How has the increasing percentage of women students on campus affected the implementation of Title IX?

7. How widespread is homophobia in sport? Has fear of lesbianism hurt the public acceptance of women's sport? Is there a difference in the treatment and perception of lesbians in sport compared to gay male athletes? Why or why not?

8. Which statement is more important in assessing athletic opportunities: Men will always be stronger and faster than women, or most men and women are more alike than different in their athletic skills?

9. The NCAA originally opposed Title IX and lobbied against it, but by 1982 it had gained authority over women's sports. What were the pros and cons of this takeover?

10. How would the history of Title IX have been different if sports like football and basketball had been excluded?

11. Are there any sports or teams that should be closed to women? Should qualified women be allowed to play on men's teams?

12. Singers, actors, and yearbook editors all add something to campus life, but are not eligible for scholarships unless they meet strict financial standards. What is the justification for athletic scholarships?

13. Has Title IX mainly benefited white women, or have women of color also benefited? What role does race play in public perceptions about sports for men and women?

14. What might happen if the "have nots" (men's minor sports and women's sports) joined together to challenge men's high-profile sports?

15. Are budgetary pressures a sufficient and compelling reason to cut teams or fail to accommodate student interests? Should women's and men's teams be treated differently when budgets need to be cut?

16. Should male athletes be able to use Title IX to sue when they feel they have been discriminated against?

17. Why are women athletes more prone to eating disorders than male athletes?

18. In 2022, Title IX will celebrate its fiftieth anniversary. Do you think the experiences and opportunities for women athletes will be much different than they are today? Will there ever be a point when laws like Title IX are no longer necessary?

Selected Bibliography

AAUW Legal Advocacy Fund. *A License for Bias: Sex Discrimination, Schools, and Title IX.* Washington, D.C.: American Association for University Women, 2000.

Birrell, Susan, and Cheryl L. Cole, eds. *Women, Sport, and Culture.* Champaign, Ill.: Human Kinetics, 1994.

Birrell, Susan, and Mary G. McDonald, eds. *Reading Sport: Critical Essays on Power and Representation.* Boston: Northeastern University Press, 2000.

Blinde, Elaine M. "Contrasting Orientation toward Sport: Pre– and Post–Title IX Athletes." *Journal of Sport & Social Issues*, 10, no. 1 (Winter/Spring 1986), 6–14.

Blumenthal, Karen. *Let Me Play: The Story of Title IX, the Law that Changed the Future of Girls in America.* New York: Atheneum Books for Young Readers, 2005.

Bowen, William G., and Sarah A. Levin. *Reclaiming the Game: College Sports and Educational Values.* Princeton, N.J.: Princeton University Press, 2003.

Brooks, Dana, and Ronald Althouse. *Racism in College Athletics: The African-American Athlete's Experience.* Morgantown, W.Va.: Fitness Information Teaching, Inc., 2000.

Byrne, Julie. *O God of Players: The Story of the Immaculata Mighty Macs.* New York: Columbia University Press, 2003.

Cahn, Susan K. *Coming on Strong: Gender and Sexuality in Twentieth-Century Women's Sport.* New York: Free Press, 1994.

Carpenter, Linda Jean. "The Impact of Title IX on Women's Intercollegiate Sports," in Arthur T. Johnson and James H. Frey, *Government and Sport: The Public Policy Issues.* Totowa, N.J.: Rowman & Allanheld, 1985.

Carpenter, Linda Jean, and R. Vivian Acosta. *Title IX.* Champaign, Ill.: Human Kinetics, 2005.

Cohen, Greta L., ed. *Women in Sport: Issues and Controversies.* Newbury Park, Calif.: Sage Publications, 1993.

Costa, D. Margaret, and Sharon Guthrie, eds. *Women and Sport: Interdisciplinary Perspectives.* Champaign, Ill.: Human Kinetics, 1994.

Festle, Mary Jo. *Playing Nice: Politics and Apologies in Women's Sports.* New York: Columbia University Press, 1996.

Gavora, Jessica. *Tilting the Playing Field: Schools, Sports, Sex and Title IX.* San Francisco: Encounter Books, 2002.

Griffin, Pat. *Strong Women, Deep Closets: Lesbians and Homophobia in Sport.* Champaign, Ill.: Human Kinetics, 1998.

Grundy, Pamela, and Susan Shackelford. *Shattering the Glass: The Remarkable History of Women's Basketball.* New York: The New Press, 2005.

Guttmann, Allen. *Women's Sports: A History.* New York: Columbia University Press, 1991.

Hall, M. Ann. *Feminism and Sporting Bodies: Essays on Theory and Practice.* Champaign, Ill.: Human Kinetics, 1996.

Hargreaves, Jennifer. *Heroines of Sport: The Politics of Difference and Identity.* New York: Routledge, 2000.

Heywood, Leslie. *Pretty Good for a Girl: An Athlete's Story.* New York: Free Press, 1998.

Heywood, Leslie, and Shari L. Dworkin. *Built to Win: The Female Athlete as Cultural Icon.* Minneapolis: University of Minnesota Press, 2003.

Jay, Kathryn. *More Than Just a Game: Sports in American Life since 1945.* New York: Columbia University Press, 2004.

Macy, Sue. *Winning Ways: A Photohistory of American Women in Sport.* New York: Henry Holt, 1996.

Mahony, Daniel F., and Donna Pastore. "Distributive Justice: An Examination of Participation Opportunities, Revenues, and Expenses at NCAA Institutions, 1973–1993." *Journal of Sport & Social Issues,* 22, no. 2 (May 1998): 127–52.

Mangan, J. A., and Roberta J. Park. *From "Fair Sex" to Feminism: Sport and the Socialization of Women in the Industrial and Post-Industrial Eras.* Totowa, N.J.: Frank Cass and Company, 1987.

McKay, Jim, Michael A. Messner, and Donald H. Sabo, eds. *Masculinities, Gender Relations, and Sport.* Thousand Oaks, Calif.: Sage Publications, 2000.

Messner, Michael A. *Power at Play: Sports and the Problem of Masculinity.* Boston: Beacon Press, 1992.

Messner, Michael A. *Taking the Field: Women, Men, and Sports.* Minneapolis: University of Minnesota Press, 2002.

Messner, Michael A., and Donald H. Sabo. *Sex, Violence & Power in Sports: Rethinking Masculinity.* Freedom, Calif.: Crossing Press, 1994.

Messner, Michael A., and Donald H. Sabo, eds. *Sport, Men, and the Gender Order: Critical Feminist Perspectives.* Champaign, Ill.: Human Kinetics, 1990.

Nelson, Mariah Burton. *Are We Winning Yet? How Women Are Changing Sports and Sports Are Changing Women.* New York: Random House, 1991.

Nelson, Mariah Burton. *The Stronger Women Get, The More Men Love Football: Sexism and the American Culture of Sports.* New York: Harcourt Brace, 1994.

Oglesby, Carole A. *Women and Sport: From Myth to Reality.* Philadelphia: Lea & Febiger, 1978.

Parkhouse, Bonnie L., and Jackie Lapin. *Women Who Win: Exercising Your Rights in Sport.* Englewood Cliffs, N.J.: Prentice-Hall, 1980.

Pemberton, Cynthia Lee A. *More Than a Game: One Woman's Fight for Gender Equity in Sport.* Boston: Northeastern University Press, 2002.

Pope, S. W., ed. *The New American Sport History: Recent Approaches and Perspectives.* Urbana: University of Illinois Press, 1997.

Porto, Brian L. *A New Season: Using Title IX to Reform College Sports.* Westport, Conn.: Praeger, 2003.

Postow, Betsy C., ed. *Women, Philosophy, and Sport: A Collection of New Essays.* Metuchen, N.J.: The Scarecrow Press, 1983.

President's Council on Physical Fitness and Sport. *Physical Activity and Sport in the Lives of Girls.* Washington, D.C.: U.S. Department of Health and Human Services, 1997.

Project on the Status and Education of Women, Association of American Colleges. *What Constitutes Equality for Women in Sport?* Washington, D.C.: Association of American Colleges, 1974.

Roberts, Randy, and James Olson. *Winning Is the Only Thing: Sports in America since 1945.* Baltimore: Johns Hopkins University Press, 1989.

Rogers, Susan Fox, ed. *Sportsdykes: Stories from On and Off the Field.* New York: St. Martin's Press, 1994.

Sabo, Don. "Women's Athletics and the Elimination of Men's Sports Programs." *Journal of Sport & Social Issues,* 22, no. 1 (February 1998): 27–31.

Sack, Allen, and Ellen J. Staurowsky. *College Athletes for Hire: The Evolution and Legacy of the NCAA's Amateur Myth.* Westport, Conn.: Praeger, 1998.

Salter, David F. *Crashing the Old Boys' Network: The Tragedies and Triumphs of Girls and Women in Sports.* Westport, Conn.: Praeger, 1996.

Sandoz, Joli, and Joby Winans, eds. *Whatever It Takes: Women on Women's Sports.* New York: Farrar, Straus and Giroux, 1999.

Shaw, Peter L. "Achieving Title IX Gender Equity in College Athletics in an Era of Fiscal Austerity." *Journal of Sport & Social Issues,* 19, no. 1 (February 1995): 6–27.

Shulman, James L., and William G. Bowen. *The Game of Life: College Sports and Educational Values.* Princeton, N.J.: Princeton University Press, 2001.

Sigelman, Lee, and Clyde Wilcox. "Public Support for Gender Equality in Athletics Programs." *Women & Politics*, 22, no. 1 (2001): 85–96.

Simon, Rita J., ed. *Sporting Equality: Title IX Thirty Years Later.* New Brunswick, N.J.: Transaction Publishing, 2005.

Smith, Lissa, ed. *Nike Is a Goddess: The History of Women in Sports.* New York: Atlantic Monthly Press, 1998.

Staurowsky, Ellen J. "Blaming the Victim: Resistance in the Battle over Gender Equity in Intercollegiate Athletics." *Journal of Sport & Social Issues*, 20, no. 2 (May 1996): 194–210.

Staurowsky, Ellen J. "Critiquing the Language of the Gender Equity Debate." *Journal of Sport & Social Issues*, 22, no. 1 (February 1998): 7–26.

Staurowsky, Ellen J. "Examining the Roots of a Gendered Division of Labor in Intercollegiate Athletics: Insights into the Gender Equity Debate." *Journal of Sport & Social Issues*, 19, no. 1 (February 1995): 28–44.

Suggs, Welch. *A Place on the Team: The Triumph and Tragedy of Title IX.* Princeton, N.J.: Princeton University Press, 2005.

Twin, Stephanie L., ed. *Out of the Bleachers: Writings on Women and Sport.* Old Westbury, N.Y.: The Feminist Press, 1979.

U.S. Commission on Civil Rights. *More Hurdles to Clear: Women and Girls in Competitive Athletics.* Washington, D.C.: U.S. Commission on Civil Rights, 1980.

U.S. Department of Education. *Title IX: 25 Years of Progress.* Washington, D.C.: U.S. Department of Education, 1997.

U.S. Department of Education, Secretary's Commission for Opportunity in Athletics. *Open to All: Title IX at Thirty.* Washington, D.C.: U.S. Department of Education, 2003.

Welch, Paula D. *Silver Era, Golden Moments: A Celebration of Ivy League Women's Athletics.* Lanham, Md.: Madison Books, 1999.

Women's Sports Foundation. *Title IX and Race in Intercollegiate Sport.* East Meadow, N.Y.: Women's Sports Foundation, 2003.

Wu, Ying. "Early NCAA Attempts at the Governance of Women's Intercollegiate Athletics, 1968–1973." *Journal of Sport History*, 26, no. 3 (Fall 1999): 585–601.

Wushanley, Ying. *Playing Nice and Losing: The Struggle for Control of Women's Intercollegiate Athletics, 1960–2000.* Syracuse: Syracuse University Press, 2004.

Acknowledgments

Ralph J. Sabock. "Football: It Pays the Bills, Son." Copyright © 1975 by The New York Times Co. Reprinted with permission.

Project on Equal Education Rights. "Stalled at the Start: Government Action on Sex Bias in the Schools." Legal Momentum, 1978.

National Collegiate Athletic Association. "Final Report of the NCAA Gender-Equity Task Force." © National Collegiate Athletic Association.

Cynthia Pemberton. *More Than a Game. One Woman's Fight for Gender Equity in Sport.* © Copyright 2002 Northeastern University Press/University Press of New England. Hanover, N.H. Reprinted with permission.

Angie Watts. "High School Athletes Talk about Gender Equity." © 1998. The *Washington Post*, reprinted with permission.

Jessica Gavora. "A Conservative Critique of Title IX." With permission from the publisher of *Tilting the Playing Field: Schools, Sports, Sex and Title IX* by Jessica Gavora, Encounter Books, San Francisco, Calif. (© 2002).

James L. Shulman, *The Game of Life.* © 2001 Princeton University Press, 2002 paperback edition. Reprinted by permission of Princeton University Press.

The Women's Sports Foundation Report: *Title IX and Race in Intercollegiate Sport* (2003).

Welch Suggs. "Title IX Has Done Little for Minority Female Athletes." Copyright 2001, the *Chronicle of Higher Education*. Reprinted with permission.

Lucy Jane Bledsoe. "Homophobia in Women's Sport." First published in the *Gay and Lesbian Review/Worldwide*.

Susan Campbell. "Cheers for Title IX." Copyright, 2005, *Hartford Courant*. Reprinted with permission.

Index

179